D1130529

# UNCOMMON CAIRO

EDITED BY

HEBA HABIB + ISABELLE MAYAULT

Copyright © Uncommon Ltd. 2015

This book is sold subject to the condition that it shall not, by way of trade or otherwise, be lent, resold, hired out, or otherwise circulated without the publisher's prior consent in any form of binding or cover other than that in which it is published and without a similar condition, including this condition, being imposed on the subsequent purchaser.

Published by Uncommon Ltd.

ISBN 978-99957-0-609-8

Printed in Italy

The opinions expressed in this book are those of the authors etc. Facts are deemed correct at time of going to print, some may be subject to change.

Managing Editor Dora Bouhara
Executive Editor Emma Mattei
Regional Editor Isabelle Mayault
Design Jon Banthorpe
Stock Photography:
p.13 Magali Corouge
p.125 Magali Corouge
p.171 Virginie Nguyen Hoang

Uncommon Ltd.
Finance House,
First Floor, Princess Elisabeth Street,
Ta' Xbiex ,
XBX 1102 Malta
www.uncommonguidebooks.com

*More than once I deserted my home city where I experienced the long and short ends of freedom. More than once I left it, embittered, enraged, determined never to see it again. More than once I abandoned it, haunted by its Citadel with its minarets, only to return again, meek and humble. To this very day, I cannot explain my inability to live in another city on the face of the earth.*

Sonallah Ibrahim, *Cairo From Edge To Edge*

# INDEX

ON THE ROAD FROM FAISAL TO TAHRIR. *MAARTJE ALDERS*

# FOREWORD

Cairo is an assault. It is big, bristling, loud and cacophonous. It is twenty million voices speaking, singing and praying at once, twenty million bodies incapable of sleep and very much inclined to dance, twenty million dreams thudding against each other, every day, without cease.

Ibn Battuta, the great Moroccan explorer, called it the 'mother of all cities' and with good reason. Cairo does not cease giving birth to things wondrous and strange, terrifying and miraculous, you could almost say that the population is cleanly split between angels and monsters. You could also say that there is every kind of hybrid of the two walking its streets, both incalculably ancient and sparklingly new.

The wonderful thing about the mother of all cities is that it is continuously being reborn, constantly shifting and contorting, to surprise and entrance you.

You could live here your entire life and still not manage to see it all, or discover all of its secrets - it is just that vast and mysterious - not to mention that you could never say with accuracy what Cairo's original face looked like. It is far too creased by countless laughter lines because that's all that keeps this overcrowded metropolis from

imploding - a great deal of laughter.

Cairo has been many places to many people: a grand Fatimid then Ottoman capital of towering mosques, bazaars, pleasure boats and palaces, the 'Paris by the Nile' conceived in grand style by the Khedive Ismail, the cosmopolitan all-embracing Hollywood of the Middle East in the forties and fifties, then the heart of the Pan Arab dream and, most recently, the site of grand social upheaval that ended with a revolution. What Cairo will become next remains to be seen but, as with all of its forms, it will doubtless continue to inspire awe, dismay and delight.

All the incarnations of Cairo linger in various forms - there for anyone willing to push through and discover more.

Uncommon Cairo is written by people who have lived or journeyed through this sleepless megacity. Here, they share what they have tasted, felt and encountered, taking us down personal routes, filled with surprise, discovery, mirage and dreams.

Uncommon Cairo will help you navigate through a complex city, not only in its geography but also in its unspoken rules (or lack of rules for Cairo is a city that thrives on structured anarchy). Made up of stories lived by those that have inhabited Cairo, here is a guide to tune in to its exhilarating frequency, an invitation to create your own story with the city.

HEBA HABIB

RELATE

# DRIFTING ON THE NILE

TEXT: **HUSSEIN EL SHAFIE**
PHOTOGRAPHY: **PASCAL MORA**

In noisy Cairo, all voices compete to break sound barriers, except one voice. The voice of the Nile, the faintest of sounds, and the pounding artery of Greater Cairo. Whenever stranded in the city, with little cash and time, felucca is the escape. These little boats keep circulating on the Cairo Nile, carrying aboard the most diverse groups of people, finding in the waters refuge from the daily burdens of land. Mina, a carpenter, Zeinab, a painter, and Sammy, a musician, sat down together to share their felucca experiences.

"Three years ago, my Russian friend and I couldn't find a place to host us because we were a boy and a girl," says Mina. "We decided to try our luck elsewhere. We went down to a garden by the Nile and decided to hire a felucca. It was late in the winter. We wanted a comfortable place to sleep and also mobility. Hag Mostafa the sailor was recommended to us. When we found him he was mending the sail. We helped him out then slept inside the felucca."

"Early morning we sailed, zigzagging through the waters, taking pictures. Sailing under bridges demonstrated Hag Mostafa's great navigation skills. We would moor the boat to islands and take walks.

At night after lighting the gas grill and making tea, we would spread the sleeping bags and sink into the starry night. There was enough space to accommodate ten people."

"I once went on a felucca ride with my friends from campus. We were singing so loud that our voices echoed off the walls of the Grand Hyatt building on the bank. We could see the reaction of the residents from the middle of the water."

"A few days ago, I wanted to ride a felucca in Zamalek. I found no sailboats so I took the one with oars. While it was sailing through the water a big party Felucca came beside it and the sailor gave us a plate of chocolate cake. It was the perfect ending for my day."

"I went to a girl-only school." says Zeinab, "My friends and I would skip classes regularly to walk to the Garden City corniche. We would chip in to buy two small packs of potato chips and, after prolonged arguing concerning the flavour selection, would jump into a felucca. We used to come up with inappropriate lyrics, compose songs and sing them, and then laughed until we gasped for air."

"While at university, I used to go out with a guy to Gezira club every day. One day he asked me: "Greenery or water?" "Water!" I answered ecstatically. He took me to a felucca, played music and lit an incense stick. I fell in love with him at that moment. The felucca took off. While sailing, we saw a silver disc-shaped object floating in the water. We could not recognise what it was and yet we were able to see the sun reflected in it. It felt like we had both the sun and the moon."

"Now whenever my friends and I want to take our dogs out, we go buy fruits and beer, take a felucca, play music and experience the healing effects of the Nile. It has become a regular recreational activity that our bodies long for from time to time. My twin sister and I celebrated our last birthday on a felucca in Maadi with some friends. We sang Shaabi music and talked about our lives."

Looking at the Nile from the shore, you don't get much, due to

the city block," says Sammy, "you can only experience the magic
from the water. You interact with the surface and watch how it reacts
with the sun and the moon. The sun-induced bright orange tinge
is a powerful source of livelihood and faith. A night on the Nile is
an entirely different journey; it is one of intuition and inspiration.
I wrote most of my last album on night felucca voyages. The dark
surface of the Nile holds infinite wisdom, and all the mysteries of the
past. I understand why the ancient Egyptians worshipped the Nile as
the male deity Hapi. It is because of the knowledge its night waters
continue to hold."

# INSIDE THE WHALE

TEXT: **AUGUSTO COMÉ**

PHOTOGRAPHY: **MAARTJE ALDERS**

Omarit Strand is its name. From taxi drivers to Cook Door Hamburgers delivery service, everybody knows this monstrous building that, like a giant cauliflower made of petrified sand, took root about fifty years ago in the heart of downtown. No need to give the house number or the name of the street, it would just confuse the visitor.

If by calling a building by its name you implicitly recognise it has a soul, I'd long been asking myself why Omarit Strand pretends to have one. After all, it's just an ordinary Cairo architectural obscenity - a collage of concrete blocks, piled up to form a makeshift building, a common representative of the architectural disaster of the Nasser Revolution, when the Paris on the Nile tried, not without certain success, to ape the style of a Southern Soviet city, like Odessa or Tashkent.

I ended up thinking that it's for this very lack of beauty and dreadful absence of striking features, like the thousands of its concrete fellows, that Omarit Strand has the privilege of bearing a name; a name to redeem them all, a name to bring them all out of the darkness and be rescued. The baptism of Omarit Strand is the redemption of all of Cairo's anonymous buildings.

If you fancy entering the building, Ahmad from Aswan is your worst enemy. You won't miss him: while speaking he shows an unsettling smile of sixteen teeth - seven of which are gold, and stretches out his wrinkled neck like an old lizard.

He is the boss of the building's six *bawabs* - the almighty doorkeepers each Cairo building is assigned. They form the intrusive battalion that protects Omarit Strand. Winning over your *bawab* is key to a pleasant routine because should he wish, he could easily turn your life into hell - he can send crooks of any sort to your flat, demanding payment of false bills, he can strand you at the twelfth floor if he has the exclusive right of driving the lift, make your visitors lose their way in the building, or let you sink in your rubbish. Having six *bawabs* is like having six mothers-in-law: it's impossible to win all of them over, no matter how good you are in gaining benevolence with tips, *as-salaam alaykums*, bowings and scrapings. As a visitor, you don't have time for this. So try to avoid them and sneak quietly towards the stairs.

Entering the building is to be swallowed by a whale. Like Pinocchio, you'll find yourself wandering in this belly of pure concrete, haunted by stray cats and dizzy patients looking for a doctor (as Omarit hosts dozens of them), but with no Geppetto to build a raft, nor wood for fire to make the whale sneeze and blast you ashore.

You can hear echoes of metallic noise, as if the building was in fact an industrial factory abandoned long ago after a barbarian invasion. As if the workers, evacuated in a rush, hadn't to switch off the engines, still spinning round, noisier and noisier, for lack of grease and maintenance.

The deeper you penetrate the building, the more frightening it becomes. With streams of cold air in your face, you have the feeling that if any of all the worst premonitions haunting you at each step would concretise, nobody would even hear your screams - no matter how excruciating they are. You start walking faster and faster, you wish to run but you don't, fearing to attract attention. Until, breathless, you reach the top floor.

It's cleaner, almost cosy. The light work and you don't hear caterwauls anymore. You'll see four doors, but you need to find the fifth one, hidden somewhere on your left. Thin, shaky stairs will lead you to the rooftop.

The sunlight blinds you. As soon as your eyes adjust, you'll find that you better watch your step. The rooftop is full of rubble and ruins, stone, brick and concrete, cast-off furniture and toys decayed by time, sun and dust. Omarit's rooftop is huge, like a central square after a quake.

From there, you'll enjoy the best urban sunset over downtown. Before the Nasser Revolution, the district was the heart of the elegant Egyptian elite. After it was colonised from the top of its buildings, derelicts coming from the remotest corners of Egypt found shelter in the capital. Since then the wealthy have vanished and moved to new and newer districts, in a constant run to isolate themselves from the rest of the world, changing downtown completely. Have-nots still live on these rooftops, hanging out their laundry, breeding their chickens, dominating their land.

You think about how good it would be to have one more can of beer, you light up your last cigarette. But really, you don't want either. You're just afraid to go through the oesophagus of the building again.

Resign yourself, there are no shortcuts, for this is how Cairo looks - shoddy stairwells, dreadful cats, shady characters and stolen moments with splendid sunsets from urban rooftops.

# THE PATH IS WHAT HE DESIRES

TEXT: AHMED AMIN
ILLUSTRATION: STEPH VON REISWITZ

I was a stone's throw away from Al Hussein Mosque, one of the most famous houses of Allah in Egypt and in the Islamic world in general. It is named after the grandson of the messenger Mohammed, as it is believed his head was finally buried in the grounds of the mosque after a torrid story of a political power struggle that ended with his decapitation, mutilation and finally his head being paraded through the streets of Kerbala.

Although the areas of Al Hussein and Khan Al Khalili, like the entirety of old Cairo, are soaked in history, it wasn't what made me go there. I was going to attend one of the Sufi circles of Zikr or vocal meditation of Al Shazleya, a way or a path in Sufism founded by Abo Al Hassan Al Shazly.

Abo el Hassan el Shazy, born in Morocco in the thirteenth century, was a learned who went on to spread his teachings in Tunisia and Egypt. His teachings centered on the transformation of consciousness to inward and outward God-centredness, contentment with God in all states, and the inner withdrawal from creation, in the best or worst of times.

It is even said that this school of Sufism had an influence on the Christian mystic Saint John of the Cross, through his encounter with Ibn Abbad el Rundi - a Moroccan adherent of the way in their accounts of the 'dark night of the soul' or the journey of the soul from its bodily home to its union with God.

Having previously worked on a short documentary about Sufism in Egypt and the various ways or paths being adopted, I had already attended meetings, witnessed circles, interviewed men and had often felt that very few were truly holy, or enlightened; but this encounter was different.

I was there, walking the same streets and standing on the same earth that once carried many great and enlightened men, a spiritual hub and an arrival terminal for many lost souls through the ages, I was looking for something deeper.

You can't receive a full message from a person without being there and feeling his presence. Quite honestly, I had decided to be at that circle of vocal meditation because I was looking for a fast food religious experience, I had hoped that I would magically feel the divine presence after chanting or whirling like a dervish. Just as one would fantasise about meditating and pronouncing the holy Om and suddenly feeling the Buddha within.

We have come to an age of instant coffee, direct sharing and addictive consumption of vast forms of media, we even think enlightenment should be instantaneous, we delight in passive and individual spiritual indulgence.

I reach the mosque - a vast place with high ceilings and verses painted around its dome in green and gold, fans whirr lazily from the ceiling and my bare feet itch from the vast woven prayer mats.

People are still filing in - old men in dusty glabeyas, young men like in jean with gelled hair, - but what united us in the same expression of deep yearning on our faces.

The *Munshid*, or the cantor, enters. We form perfect concentric circles and join hands to enter this circle watched by angels - a circle that will take us beyond our lives and sense the deep radiance that is within and outside us.

The *Munshid's* deep sonorous voice begins to chant the *Ibitihalat* (entreaties to God) and then the poetry of praising the beloved - the one we all seek union with. Drums play and we move together. Not quite dancing but accompanying the poetry with our feet as if we were entering it, entering the praise with our bodies, we are unified by this moment.

This was not quite what I was looking for - it is more than that. It is dizzying and not easy, but I try to listen to the words that invoke *'Galalet el Ism'* or the glory of the name of God.

There is terror at first - this sense of losing yourself in the moment but then you become more deeply aware: you are you and everyone else, there is great peace when you submit to the movement and echo everyone else.

Later I meet with the Sheikh who led the circle and am entranced by his quiet grace, his modesty and his eloquence. It is not a long encounter but it teaches me a great deal.

He tells me that he has reached this state not because he read a lot, or had unflawed logic or solely because he prayed, chanted and meditated. It was rather the cumulative toll his steps have taken on his soul. His path has no end. He isn't aimed at going anywhere or finding anything. He simply wants to exist and remain on the path; it's the path itself that will bring the love, the joy and even the peace, not the ultimate prize or final destination.

He said, "If I go to *Janna* (Paradise/Heaven) it is not because I had it in mind as a destination or goal, but because working towards being present in my present was fulfilling. Being on the path, taking the road of worship and love enables me to exist in the void."

The path itself is what he desires, not the destination. That is the true lesson.

A city walked on foot will teach you more than a book. Being present and aware of one's life and size in comparison to our surroundings, starting from the ant and ending with God is the only way to a full and real existence.

# THE TRAVELLING LENS

TEXT: **WAEL ISKANDAR**

PHOTOGRAPHY: **MOSIREEN COLLECTIVE**

Streets can be empty even when they're bustling with activity. The normalcy of streets, as crowded as they may be, is a sort of nothingness waiting to be transformed into something. As people go about their business on the street, their purpose differs and yet the street brings them together. The purpose must not be undermined. It is a sense of collective purpose to occupy those streets and change their normalcy into protest that gave birth to the revolution.

It is the magic of turning that nothingness of normalcy into something purposeful that captures my heart particularly with the Kazeboon street screenings. In the past I had walked into these screenings after the magic had vanished. The screens had been set up, the power supply had been accounted for, the show was running and the people had gathered. This time around, I was a part of it. There's something different about being part of the magic as it is being created, being part of the transformative process that changes the utility of the street to something of your own making, a platform for dissent.

I toured Cairo's streets and saw the city through a different lens. It's a transformative lens that physically changed those streets. Each neighbourhood brought its own struggles and dynamics. In seeing the streets through Kazeboon's lens, it seemed that the projections on the walls or bed sheets were transforming the streets into another Tahrir Square. They were transporting the revolution that aimed to uncover the truth to a place that had not been willing to be transformed; places which chose to ignore what had happened in other streets.

One of the most unforgettable screenings was in April 2013, underneath Kareka's house in Nasr City. Mohamed Mostafa (Kareka) was a young, talented man from a middle-class family who was truly dedicated to revolutionary ideals. He was a tennis champion, a swimmer and an Ahly Ultras fan. He was killed by the military in December 2011 during the Cabinet Attacks, and his mother was promised retribution by Morsi personally, but never followed through.

Our goal, when arriving at the scene outside Kareka's house, was to set up the screen before the march arrived. The street had nothing remarkable: a few shops open, mostly residential homes and a slow traffic flow. Finding the perfect spot for a screen means, first of all, to locate a power supply. Street lights generally do the trick but, in this case, the nearest one was not working, so electricity had to be taken from elsewhere. Some suggested we use the electricity outlet of a closed a shop but we never steal electricity from private properties without asking, so, graciously, neighbors allowed us to connect to their power supply. Another key element for a screen is to make sure the audience can see and feel comfortable without blocking traffic, something that often requires ingenious thinking in Cairo's tightly designed streets, where no free space is left unutilized.

As we were setting up, a man came up to ask us what we were doing, we told him that this was Kareka's house and that we were screening in tribute to him. He responded that he didn't know that one of the martyrs of the revolution had lived on their street.

As the screenings started, many of Kareka's friends, neighbours and family were present. Lie after lie was screened and all the broken promises were collectively difficult to bear. Then came the broken promise of bringing the guilty to justice. A film was screened so was a collection of his photos and footage of him captured during his lifetime. It showed his dedication to justice and revolutionary ideals. Everyone cried at the loss. The loss of a friend, a brother, a son and a comrade; he was killed by an army that was supposed to protect him, like many others.

In late December 2012 there was another unforgettable screening near Jika's house. Mohamed Gaber (Jika) was killed by the police under Morsi. He lived in Abdeen, a neighbourhood that had previously been hostile to any revolutionary activities. Yet this time around people were welcoming and accommodating the screenings. The effect of the screening had similar affects to the event organised around Jika's life, his friends, young revolutionaries were moved to tears. The scene was intense, with a strong sense of injustice and yet there was defiance, but most of all there was a lot of love for a wonderful young man who chose not to be silenced and paid the price. You can see the passion through the angry chants, the sad faces and the tears that flowed almost endlessly. Jika's father, Gaber, spoke in between the film screenings. He spoke lovingly about his son to people's minds and hearts. The street that felt alienating to us as we marched through it, suddenly felt like home.

Neighbourhoods have a different taste to them when doing something connected to the country as a whole. That is the unifying experience of the revolution, where locally everyone is doing something global. There have been close to a thousand Kazeboon street screenings since its inception, even outside Egypt. I've witnessed similar transformations in places like Maadi, Dokki, Sayeda Aisha and many other neighbourhoods. Each neighbourhood has its story, every screening is different. Some are more violent than others, some more successful than others.

Yet it is through this travelling lens that I can see what places can be, in just a few minutes - how they can transform. I can't help but wonder if this lens has uncovered the truth for me or added another layer to reality.

KAZEBOON (LIARS) IS A COLLECTIVE OF ACTIVISTS WHO HOSTED A SERIES OF SCREENINGS SHOWING POLICE VIOLENCE IN VARIOUS NEIGHBOURHOODS, AS A WAY TO OCCUPY PUBLIC SPACE AND CREATE PUBLIC DEBATE. WAEL ISKANDAR IS ONE OF THE FOUNDERS OF THE COLLECTIVE. THIS TEXT AIMS TO DESCRIBE THE IMMEDIATE POST-REVOLUTIONARY PERIOD - HOW CAIRO WAS AT THAT VERY MOMENT, HOW PEOPLE TALKED AND WHAT THEY WERE TALKING ABOUT.

# FAR WEST

TEXT: **LAURA DEAN**
PHOTOGRAPHY: **FRANÇOISE BEAUGUION**

6th of October City is many things to many people. To wealthy compound dwellers it's a haven, away from the din and dust of the city, behind the high walls that separate them from those who would otherwise be their neighbours. To migrants from the provinces, it's a place to come to find work in its numerous factories. To the former residents of Duweiqa, it is a patch of desert where they are marooned, waiting endlessly to be resettled somewhere closer to their home neighbourhood in the city centre. To students from around the Arab world who attend one of the thirteen private universities, it's a means to a degree and a better life back home. To the glittering media elite, it's where to film episodes of their latest talk shows and soap operas. To Syrian and other refugees, it's a place to live together in a community, until it's safe to make their way back to Damascus, Baghdad, Khartoum, or anywhere the city's diverse residents might call home.

As you drive out toward 6th of October City, you get a view of the brick and concrete reasons why it was built in the first place. The fertile river-fed soil at the edge of the Nile is protected farmland. However, in the 1970s, during the presidency of Anwar Sadat, as housing in the city centre grew harder to come by, people began to build on it. Older Cairenes often describe the Giza fields "stretching out toward the pyramids." These days oblong brick tubes stick out of embattled grassy strips, rebars left poking out of the top aspirationally, in case money comes through to build a new floor.

Sadat's supremely modernist solution was to build a new city in the desert by presidential decree in 1976, in hopes that people would seek homes out there instead of on increasingly scarce farmland. Thus 6th of October City was born. It takes its name from the date when Egypt made significant advances during the October War of the Arab-Israeli conflict in 1973. The dream of conquering the desert has been around since Pharaonic times, and 6th of October City was one of the first attempts.

With residential neighbourhoods, commercial centres and an industrial area, it was meant to be a self-contained community in the desert. There are a few official bus routes, but the most efficient way to get around is by microbus or pick-up truck on the main streets, and by tuk tuk (auto-rickshaw) in the narrower areas. Out here even the weather is different: in the desert, it tends to be hotter during the day and cooler at night.

Driving in from Cairo, one is greeted by billboards advertising the life that's possible out here, beyond the cramped hustle of the city. *You'll enjoy yourself* promises one sign. Another advertises *London Tennis*, next to it is a spinning three-dimensional golf ball. Space is not at a premium out here - it is perhaps what the desert has the most of - so such sports are possible at 6th of October City. Luxury compounds cluster at the entrance - in one, each house is a Mediterranean-style villa with red-orange tiled roofs and whitewashed walls. The next advertises itself as '*the community of champions*'. Yet as central Cairo pushes out towards the desert, the boundaries between the two cities grow increasingly blurred and here, as in the city centre, the traffic moves in, stops and starts.

Out here malls are the main places to go to unwind after a week's work and before the uprisings, several more were slated to be built. Many projects have been on hold since 2011.

In addition to spaces dedicated to consumption, 6th of October is full of subsidised housing, or at least it was intended to be. Unemployment among young men meant that many could not afford to get married and start a family. Instead of focusing on creating jobs, the government solution to this chronic late twentieth century problem was a built one: in places like 6th of October much of the housing is supposed to be reserved for young families. But the system is rife with corruption, and it's far more lucrative to sell these apartments to the highest bidder than to use them for their intended purpose.

In the 1990s, the government decided to bring in the private sector to help develop the land, with middling success. A large chunk of 6th of October, intended to be mixed-income housing is now Dreamland, a development with two five-star hotels, luxury residential compounds, an amusement park and a golf course.

Then there are the ghost towns. Build Your Own House is a 'scheme' - the government provides the land and a few basic services: water, electricity, sewage, and people build their houses themselves. However, the guard at the entrance, who commutes from central Cairo every week, says that people have begun to despair: "It's just too far out in the desert. Too far from schools, from shops, from life."

There are thirteen private universities in 6th of October. Most of the students come from Palestine, Jordan and Syria, with a few Iraqis and Saudis thrown in, judging by the array of Arabic accents. For many, it's a guaranteed means of getting a degree, so that they can get a job in their home country.

The UN Refuge Agency has one of its major offices in 6th of October, and successive waves of refugee communities have made it their home. Most recently, Little Baghdad became Little Damascus. Today if you go to Hossari Square you will find it filled with young Syrians playing billiards and selling Syrian-made goods, sitting in restaurants serving delicious shawerma and mana'eesh.

6th of October was once its own province but since 2011, it has been swallowed up again by the ever-expanding urban beast that is central Cairo. In the showrooms of the large developers you can see that they have big dreams for the city in the desert. But piles of brown and grey sand, rebar and concrete suggest they have some way to go. After two and a half years of upheaval, many people here are anxious to return to some measure of stability, at least for long enough to finish a few construction projects.

# A DAY AT THE MUSEUM

TEXT: MONICA HANNA

ILLUSTRATION: HICHAM RAHMA

The Egyptian Museum in Cairo is a museum of a museum; inaugurated in 1902, its display has changed little over time. The French architect, Marcel Dougnon, designed it in the neo-classical style. The collection has around 120,000 objects from the Predynastic until the Coptic Period, thus covering the entire ancient Egyptian history. It has a basement used as storage for many objects. The museum is open every day from 9am to 7pm.

Unfortunately, no photos are allowed inside the museum, but that is a very good chance to spend more time absorbing the immensity of such a rich collection. Visitors who are not part of large groups are advised to take time to begin their visit downstairs with the Predynastic period. The museum visit moves clockwise, and then you go upstairs to visit the Tutankhmun collection, and the royal and animal mummies, among many other things.

Ancient Egypt is one of the most solid historical periods in world civilisation. It produced significant art, science, literature and technology that have affected the whole world. The climatic and geological conditions in Ancient Egypt helped the state of stability because the River Nile flows from South to North, while the wind blows from North to South, which helped navigation on the river. In addition, the inundation seasons were concurrent with the agricultural seasons. This helped a magnificent culture to flourish, enjoying long-term political stability, compared to its neighbours, on the banks of the longest rivers in the world. The Egyptian Museum in Cairo tries to capture the glimpses of such a vast historical period through the different objects on display. It is considered the most complete collection of Egyptian archaeology in the world.

Evidence of civilization in Ancient Egypt is dated back to prior the Neolithic period (5100-3900 BCE). Around the time of the Naqada III (3150 BCE), which is considered the Protodynastic period, Egypt is unified into a state under the King Narmer, with the main cemetery in Abydos. Then the capital of Egypt moved to Memphis, which lead to the start of the Old Kingdom. Afterwards comes the period of the Pyramids, and as the uncommon Arabic proverb says, 'Everything is afraid of time, yet time is afraid of the pyramids'. The Cairo Museum houses spectacular sculpture coming from the Giza plateau, Saqqara and Dahshur dating to this time. This period was characterised by the formation of the first Egyptian artistic styles, translating everything that in the early Dynasty Period was built of mud, to stone.

By the end of the Old Kingdom as King Pepi II grew old and weak, the provincial governors gained stronger power. Egyptian unity disintegrated and from the dynasties 7-10, ranging around 350 years, Egypt fell into civil unrest with two different central powers in Ihnasiya (Heracleopolis) and Thebes.

Finally, the Theban leader Mentuhotep II reunites Egypt and the Middle Kingdom begins, with changes in art and architecture. Royal funerary construction becomes humbler than that of the Old Kingdom, and pyramids are built on a smaller scale in Dahshur, Lisht, Beni Suef and Fayoum. The earlier Pyramid Texts evolve into Coffin Texts and are used by a broader public, not just by the rulers. During the Middle Kingdom, the irrigation system of Egypt is engineered, along with its bureaucratic government form.

After such an organised period, Egypt falls again into the mayhem of civil war and a weak political situation develops. The Delta is infiltrated by Levantine populations, locally called the Hyksos, who take control of Lower Egypt. They come with horses, and use new war technologies, such as composite bows and chariots, throughout dynasties fifteen and sixteen (1650-1550 BCE). Their capital locations are Avaris and Qantir. This results in the division of Egypt into the Northern rule under foreigners and Southern rule under Theban princes. The material culture of the Hyksos is quite rare as its cultural diffusion was limited and their sites are still under excavation. In the South, Theban rulers solidified power and by the end of the Second Intermediate Period, tension escalates and war breaks out under the reigns of Seqnenre, Kamose and Ahmose. They manage to expel the Hyksos and reunite the country. Women of that period, such as Queens Ahhotep and Ahmose Nefertari, have their prominent role in the liberation war.

The first part of the New Kingdom was a period of internal stabilisation and firmer control over areas beyond historical borders, particularly during the reigns of Tuthmosis I to Tuthmosis III (1524-1424 BCE). Nubia, already under the control of a viceroy, is completely subjugated. Palestine and Southern Syria are administered by Egyptian commissaries, while the rest of the small principalities of the Near East are dependents of Egypt. The military expansion became an economic power and a cultural supremacy, allowing Egypt in the New Kingdom to reach the peak of its artistic production and giving life to an extremely sophisticated civilization. In this context, there is the story of Hatchepsut (1472-1457 BCE) wife of Tuthmosis II and co-regent of Tuthmosis III. A good deal of the richness conquered under the military campaigns is donated to the

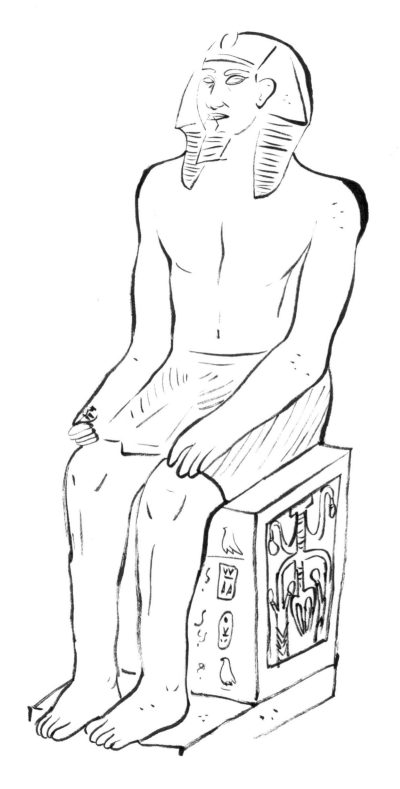

Temple of Amun in Thebes. The priests in these temples administer huge properties and gain more and more power, posing a threat to the King himself. The religious policy of the father and grandfather is brought to its extreme by Amenhotep IV, who promotes a monotheism that is more or less centered around the sun-disk (Aten), and forces the closure of the traditional temples.

This religious reform had a long lasting influence on art and literature and did not survive the King. Traditional religion is restored after his death, although enriched by elements of personal piety, previously unknown. At the end of the 18th Dynasty there is a change of bloodline and the founder of the 19th Dynasty is the general of the army Ramesses I (1298-1296 BCE). His son Seti I (1296-1279 BCE) and his grandson Ramesses II (1279-1212 BCE) bring Egypt back to the glory of the 18th Dynasty, with intense construction, commercial and military activity. The capital city is moved to the Delta (Per Ramesses), a city built from scratch.

It is evident that political access now moved North. During the Amarna Period, the supremacy of Egypt over the satellite states of Syria and Palestine is successfully challenged by another imperial power - the Hittites. The final battle is fought in Qadesh. Both sides may claim victory, but it leads to the end of Egyptian expansion and implements peace. Shortly after, the invasion of the so-called Sea People crashed the Hittite Empire and the prosperity of the Syria-Palestine principalities. Only Egypt, during the reign of Ramesses III (1185- 1153 BCE), opposes the resistance and is not destroyed. The sovereign is remembered in a papyrus that records a labor strike by Valley of the Kings' workers, who protested against a delay in payments. Despite the relative splendour of Ramesses III's reign, this is sympotmatic of the economic crisis caused by the political collapse of the Near East and Anatolia, which Egypt could not avoid. The subsequent monarchs, almost all called Ramesses until Ramesses XI (1094-1064 BCE), did not sparkle with fame. Moreover, the New

Kingdom ends amongst attempts of revolt, the manoeuvre of the clergy of Amun, and a deep economic crisis.

The Third Intermediate Period starts after the death of Ramesses XI, and is considered a period of decline and political stability, where Egypt is ruled by foreigners. The priests of Amun in Thebes become more powerful and rule Upper and Middle Egypt in the twenty first dynasty, while King Smendes I rules lower Egypt from the city of Tanis.

Then starts what is known as the Libyan Period founded by Shoshenq I in 945 BCE. He unifies Egypt for around 100 years, but after the reign of Osorkon II, Egypt fell into two lands again. The women of this dynasty are also proclaimed as the God's wives of Amun in Thebes.

During the twenty-fourth dynasty, the Kushite King Kashta expels Amenerdis and installs his daughter as the successor of the God's wife of Amun, and slowly spreads power through Egypt. By the twenty-fifth dynasty, King Piye establishes a strong hold in Egypt and it is reunited again under the reign of King Taharqa, who restores the Temples. However, the dynasty soon falls apart and the rulers retreat to Napata. The international influence of Egypt withdraws and by 664 BCE Egypt falls to the Assyrians.

The dynasty of King Psmatik I, the 26th dynasty (664 - 525 BCE), ended with the rule of Ahmose II (570 - 526 BCE), whose death was shortly followed by the invasion of Egypt by Persian King Cambyses.

After this period, the Saïte Period begins and Egypt sufferes instability until Alexander the Great occupies Egypt in 332 BCE and establishes the rule of the Ptolemaic Period that ends with Cleopatra VII, who lost Egypt in battle against the Romans in 30 BCE.

Art in Ancient Egypt in all eras served purposes other than that of artistic expression. It acted as a strong visual representation of power of the different political periods in addition to playing a role in the cosmic order of Ancient Egypt. Art did not exist in a vacuum as we see it today in the museum. This can be observed as early as the fourth millennium BCE through the few objects found dating to the Naqada and Badrian Predynastic cultures. Objects like slate palettes, combs, votive objects and others reveal the artists intent to observe his environment and transfer it to earthenware.

The objects also served a religious purpose , preserving images of this life to remind the deceased of it in the afterlife. This was a reflection of Ancient Egyptian beliefs regarding rebirth and resurrection in the afterlife and the driving force for the creation of the first funerary decorations made of organic material that was later translated to stone.

# EL AHRAMAT

PHOTOGRAPHY: **LAURA EL-TANTAWY**

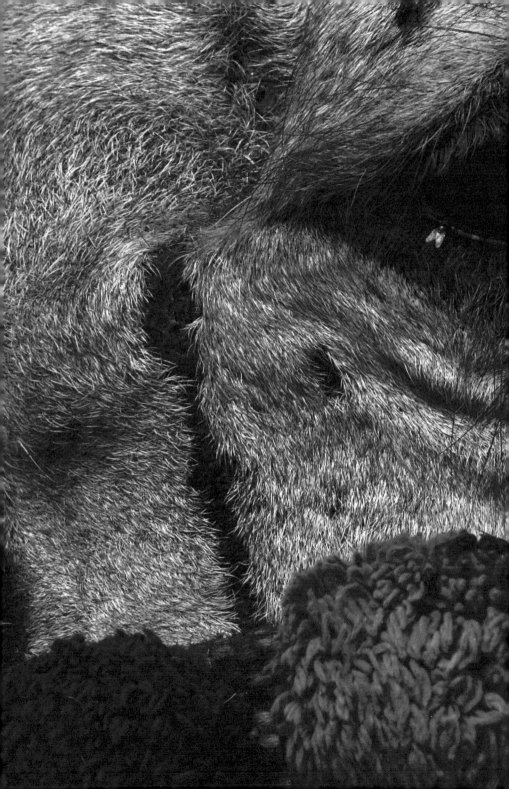

# THE TORN PHOTO

TEXT: **MARIAM SAADELDIN**

PHOTO: **PASCAL MORA**

As a child, I was intrigued by my grandmother's personal stuff. Being raised in an old high-ceiling Art Deco apartment in Zamalek with plenty of doors, old armoires and locked closets, I felt like Alice in my grandmother's wonderland.

There was a combination of scents in her room, a mixture of old books, her cigarettes, the salt she put in water to heal her feet after long walks as a tourist guide. Her old vintage cushions and linens linger with me to this day - along with stories of her youth that make me feel like I belong to the wrong era. Perhaps those stories are what made me want to become a filmmaker.

One day amongst my aunt's belongings I found an old black and white photograph of one of my favourite actresses, a beauty icon, dating back to the sixties. I noticed it was torn and repaired with old tape - after probing my dad, I discovered that after a fight with my aunt, my grandma had torn the photo off the wall and ripped it as punishment. The story never left my mind for some reason.

Four years later, in 1999, during my last year at the Higher Cinema Institute, I was working on a short film for my graduation. I had written a story of bonding between a young girl and an old lady that takes place on a plane. I won't lie to you - *she* was on my mind, I felt the role was perfect for her, the 1960s icon and actress.

But I had trouble enough sorting out permission to film on a plane and at the Cairo airport, I didn't need more trouble or disappointments; yet somehow my production manager procured her telephone number: Joy! Terror!

I called her in a crowded street, so she wouldn't hear my apprehension. She answered - how different her voice was to the one on screen! To my surprise she was gracious and welcoming. I took her address.

I was too shy to go by myself, so my production manager and I reached her place in Garden City, Cairo. A lovely old building, a street surrounded by trees, I guess that's where the street name comes from (*Sharia Nabatat*, means 'Plant Street'). We asked the *bawab* for the apartment, he told us it was located on the last floor. I couldn't feel my knees as the elevator took us up. Once on her floor, we found a huge portrait of her on the wall and something written on it *Gama3eyet El Hemeer* which means 'The Donkeys Club', a group she created a long time ago for cinema artists.

I rang the door bell, she opened the door and greeted us. I remember feeling like the luckiest person in the world. Forgive me for not being able to describe her apartment in detail, this is something that happened fifteen years ago after all. But I do remember a portrait of her signed by an extremely talented film director who was a painter too, a photo of her in one of the most famous movies in Egypt's history, and the old wooden stairs leading to the roof.

I was in a daze. Here I was, before one of the most important actresses of Egyptian cinema - a cool blonde who could have easily been cast by Hitchcock. She had diminished - there was no denying it. From a screen goddess she had become a modest looking lady in her late seventies, but I was thrilled. If I managed to cast her, doubtless my little film would become one of the best ever made at the institute.

As soon as I explained my film to her, the arguments began, she criticised it in every way imaginable. I was crushed.

I left feeling that I was dealing with an extremely high-maintenance person. But no one can judge her for that, after all, she worked with the most important film directors. She was supposed to call me in the upcoming days, because the airport permits meant we were short on time.

Nerve-wracking times! My father came to my room and told me that *she* was on the phone. We laughed, it was ridiculous that this screen goddess was calling a student! I picked up and she said, "Listen, I am calling you to tell you that I might disappear for a couple of days, I am leaving the city." She hung up saying she would call me upon her return.

Two more days, and to my surprise, she called back, we met again, but this time I went alone. I can't remember how many hours I spent there, talking and mostly arguing because she wanted to change the whole plot of my script! On that day I noticed for the first time that there were beer bottle caps all over the floor. She kept on drinking all through our conversation. Her ashtrays were filled to the brim with cigarette stubs - it shocked me.

She let me stare at her picture, the one with her favourite role, and she sat close to me, really close, and put her hand on my shoulder and said, you remind me of one of my favourite directors Shady Abdel Salam. I felt really flattered, I couldn't speak after what she said, but I decided to share the torn photo story with her.

She left to the kitchen and got me a wrapped chocolate egg, the Easter ones with a toy inside from Simonds (a well-known patisserie in Egypt). She held the egg and stared at me and said, "Do you know what's inside the egg?" I said no, she continued, "It might be a bird or a dinosaur... Do you want to be a bird or a dinosaur Louisa?" (Louisa was a character she played).

I admit, at the age of twenty that was way too philosophical for me, so I insisted on her final decision. It ended up with both of us being stubborn and not finding a middle ground: she didn't mind acting in a short film, but she wanted to change the whole script. I asked her to think about it and that I would call her the next day.

The next day was my last phone call to her, she was quite irritated by me, I guess it was mutual. I apologised that I couldn't change my script and I thanked her for her time, but surprisingly *she* said "why don't you call MF?"

MF was a well-known actress, still living, but known for her shocking opinions and foul mouth.

Now, at the age of thirty-six, looking back at that week, remembering how serious I was about my project, I've come to realise that *she*, I guess, was playing... Now, I think she wanted to play those little games adults enjoy to play, especially with younger people. She knew she was teaching me something, she knew she would forget about it completely.

REVIEW

# DUST

PHOTOGRAPHY: **XENIA NIKOLSKAYA**

Only someone with a background in archaeology could attempt to document the empty spaces of cosmopolitan Cairo as thoroughly as photographer Xenia Nikolskaya did. For six years she has explored and documented the long-forgotten palaces, built between 1840 and 1960, looking for what has gone missing, and what remains.

**SAKAKINI PALACE, CAIRO, 2007**
THE PLASTIC CHAIRS ARE LEFTOVERS OF
THE DAYS WHEN THE PALACE WAS PART OF
THE MEDICAL MUSEUM. WHEN THE PASHA
DIED, ONE OF SAKAKINI'S GRANDSONS
OFFERED THE PALACE TO THE MINISTRY OF
HEALTH AS A WAY OF CONTRIBUTING TO THE
PROFESSION - FOR HE WAS A DOCTOR.

**VILLA CASDAGLI, GARDEN CITY, CAIRO, 2010**
VILLA CASDAGLI WAS BUILT DURING THE FIRST
DECADE OF THE 20TH CENTURY BY AUSTRIAN
ARCHITECT EDWARD MATASEK FOR EMANUEL
CASDAGLI, A BRITISH-EDUCATED LEVANTINE
MERCHANT WHO HAD DEALINGS IN THE
LUCRATIVE TEXTILE TRADE IN MANCHESTER.
POSSIBLY, THE HOUSE WAS ORIGINALLY BUILT
FOR BANKER FELIX SUARES AND FOLLOWING
HIS DEATH IN APRIL 1906, WAS SOLD TO THE
CASDAGLIS IN 1909.

**BIG HALL, THE NATIONAL GEOGRAPHIC SOCIETY MUSEUM, CAIRO, 2010**

THE SOCIETY WAS FOUNDED BY KHEDIVE ISMAIL ON THE 19TH OF MAY 1875 AS AN INDEPENDENT ORGANISATION LOCATED IN THE EL SHURA COUNCIL COMPOUND IN KASR EL AINI STREET. THIS BIG HALL IS USED FOR THE SOCIETY MEETINGS.

لخطر القاهرة
قاربت الوراق
اروح بسامى
ريقيا توفى
حمد توفى : ايمن شمعه
I A
N

**BARON D'EMPAIN PALACE,
HELIOPOLIS, CAIRO, 2011**
BARON D'EMPAIN PALACE (QASR AL BARON)
WAS INSPIRED BY THE ANGKOR WAT TEMPLE
IN CAMBODIA AND HINDU TEMPLES IN
ORISSA, INDIA. IT WAS BUILT BY THE FRENCH
ARCHITECT, ALEXANDER MARCEL, AND
DECORATED BY GEORGES-LOUIS CLAUDE.
CONSTRUCTION WAS COMPLETED IN 1911. IT IS
BELIEVED THAT ALL THE HINDU PIECES WERE
BROUGHT FROM INDIA.

RADIO CINEMA, CAIRO, 2010

RADIO CINEMA USED TO BE ONE OF THE PREMIER
MOVIE THEATRES OF MIDDLE EASTERN CINEMA.
SINCE CINEMA PRODUCTION IN EGYPT HAS
DROPPED FROM FOUR HUNDRED TO FOUR FILMS
PER YEAR, THERE IS NO LONGER A NEED FOR SO
MANY CINEMAS IN CAIRO.

# THE PROSE POETRY OF NASR CITY

TEXT: SVEN KARNGÅRD

Are these asteroids in space, with angels and demons fluttering about, lit up by city stars and other celestial bodies? The cars, circling these blocks forever - you can find drivers who haven't been home since the dawn of the universe - are spaceships in orbit, making cosmic music with their horns and forever missing the right exit. Taxi metres counting out light-years in pounds.

There is a kind of Gothic steam punk quality about the battered facades of Nasr City. The desert storms are blasting the concrete with the hand of a rather rough artist, giving it the patina and air of a late twentieth century version of Dickens' London or the Paris of Zola. The sand has distorted some of the gloomily majestic buildings to such an extent they seem only part man-made, wild and dramatic.

Adding to the romanticism are the heavily gilt and luxuriously tinted homes, all gold, indigo, rose, hidden away inside these sandstone pillars, the meticulously polished pride of pedantic Nasrian women and their helpers.

Civilization is not the conquest of nature by square minds to create practical and comfortable environments, but rather interior decorators subduing nature under the marvellously impractical and beautiful, with or without style and taste.

Termite mounds with little Versailles flats inside. Or perhaps: the glimpse of an open window as you flash past in a taxi gives the impression of a dried up coral reef, which will burst into dazzling colours once submerged in water, or radiant desert flowers waiting for the rains.

And the dear little flying creatures: military helicopters buzzing, jet fighters roaring, such busy bees over these stern cacti! You only see them in town, as they are shy to the dangers of the wilderness beyond.

In bureaucratic prose, this vast area exactly equals the Million Program areas in the country I'm growing away from, Sweden, yet they are different in poetical essence: the Swedish conformist sensibility turns the very air gray, while the Egyptian concrete is infused with desert sand magic.

Projections of a tourist with excess luggage of romanticism. A mythology no less suspect than those of the inhabitants, neither more. Or, if the vision is not the truth, revealed to me alone, why not a mirage in the burning sun and shisha smoke. I need another lemonade - this place is looking enchanted again!

Dull scholars who see death and danger in romanticism and exoticism - do they marry for objective reasons? Is it objectively true that these are not sandcastles longing for distant oceans, or should we hand the dullards pail and shovel?

These banks of oysters and clams, with decrepit elevators and Salafis forcing grim decency upon the juicy pearls. The cleaning lady is not impressed with my likening of marble floors to mother of pearl; not her kind of romanticism after scrubbing them for decades. Still, she is born and bred here, and these buildings shine with poetry in her eyes as well. A busy bee who knows her flowers and hives. The prose poetry of Nasr City added in translucent layer on layer, until these buildings are enveloped in a haze of stories as impenetrable to the gaze as the orange sandstorm clouds.

Veiled glittering beetles for Orientalist entomologists; bearded squids in white *galabeyas*, a little inky about the hem. We are here like playful fish or little confused butterflies between these serious walls.

# MUSEUM OF FOUND OBJECTS

TEXT + PHOTOGRAPHY: **MIRJAM LINSCHOOTEN + SAMEER FAROOQ**

When the car drove us through nocturnal Cairo along wide cosmopolitan boulevards lined with bright neon signs, nothing seemed out of the ordinary. Until suddenly we exited the ring road and entered a dense grid of unpaved roads, apartment buildings and streets crammed with tuk tuks, watermelon pyramids, donkey-carts and every other imaginable street impediment. Here was a completely different Cairo than what we had imagined: Ard El Lewa.

During a six-week residency in June and July 2013, we were going to pursue our project *The Museum of Found Objects* (started in Istanbul in 2010) at Artellewa Art Space. It was our first stay in Cairo, a city that had been making headlines for the past two years. We expected to feel a sense of familiarity for this place that had been reported about so extensively. Instead, the unanticipated reality of daily life immediately took over. The experience of living and working in Ard El Lewa became just as much part of the project as questioning the notion of value we place on objects.

Artellewa Art Space was founded in 2007 by artist Hamdy Reda. Born and raised in Ard El Lewa, one of his goals is to bring together different cultures by inviting foreign artists to work with and among the community. Artellewa consists of three separate spaces: two galleries and a large studio space for weekly movie screenings and presentations, seemingly out of place - as though three white cubes landed on a dusty road. We set up our workspace in one of the galleries. Its large windows overlooking the street also created a visual dialogue: we watched people in the neighbourhood passing by and they watched us working inside.

The starting point for *The Museum of Found Objects Cairo* was a compelling image from the Egyptian Revolution of 2011 - when citizens of Cairo formed a human chain around the Egyptian Museum on Tahrir Square to protect its priceless contents from being looted. Still, according to a document issued by Egypt's Supreme Council of Antiques, approximately fifty four items were stolen or damaged. With everyday objects as the central point of our exploration, it presented an interesting opportunity to analyse what we deem valuable.

Unlike our previous museums in Istanbul and Toronto, this time we set out to engage the public in our process of collecting. We erected a pop-up photo studio sourced from materials in the area and worked with a local calligrapher to make announcement posters welcoming residents to bring us their objects. We asked a simple question: *What personal object would you like to see displayed in the Egyptian Museum?*

We were unsure whether anyone would come in - would the barrier be too high? However, during our opening hours a variety of people of different ages and backgrounds came by, out of curiosity, or to bring us their objects.

We asked each person a series of questions, delving deeper into the underlying reasons for their choices. Some people chose a practical device, such as Gannah who brought us her mobile phone, which keeps her connected to her friends, while others opted for objects of sentimental value, like the broken glass Abdul brought us - a reminder of the girl he loved. Men walked in more easily than women, who remained reserved. In an effort to approach the female community Mirjam went for a haircut at local hairdresser Donia, who owns a women's hair salon next to Artellewa. Donia not only introduced her to other women and offered her a facial treatment, but also brought us her wedding jewellery to photograph.

During these hours we'd often pull out some chairs and place them in front of the gallery, which created valuable moments of spontaneous dialogue. Discussions around objects would often turn into larger debates around the current political situation.

While photographing an object, the electricity would suddenly cut out; or, in trying to reach a neighbourhood to collect a particular item, we would be stuck behind a line of cars waiting to fill their tanks during an acute petrol shortage. Within the context of the furious politics surrounding us, there was an absurdity to photographing a piece of bread, a plastic comb or a mobile phone. But we felt it was important to speak for these everyday objects that were no less significant than the political discussions underway at the time.

## FOWL

At the Egyptian Museum many animal-related objects are on display, including an entire section of animal mummies.

Daily life in Cairo is full of animals too. Cats are everywhere: coming down staircases, sitting atop cars, or sleeping in the waiting room between applicants for visa extensions. Additionally, many Egyptians keep various fowl on their rooftops for consumption. Mohamed let us borrow one of his roosters to be photographed. It was described as a very calm Egyptian variety, and mostly stayed glued in a corner of the box trying to make sense of its reflection. What would it tell its peers when it returned to the roof - that it had had a bad dream?

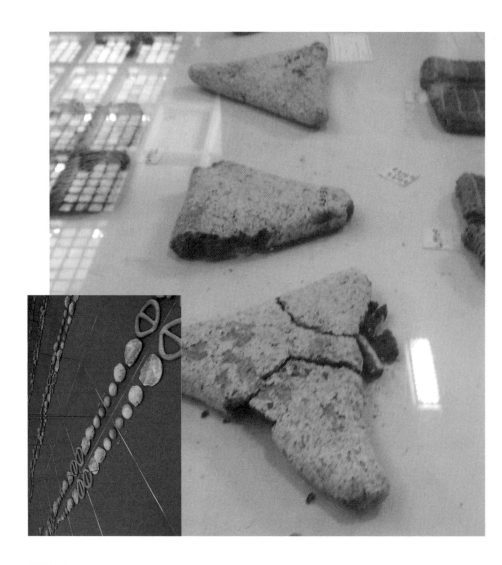

**BREAD**

'Three cornered' loaves of bread lay perfectly preserved in a case on the second floor of the Egyptian Museum. Surprisingly, these loaves of bread have been with us since the eleventh dynasty of Ancient Egypt (Dynasty XI) from Thebes. Parallel to them is a variety of breads from Shohada Street in Ard El Lewa, including eish masri, aish merahrah, fiteer, and smeet.

Bread is often transported by bicycle with the delivery person carrying a very large basket atop their head.

C. 44048
Silver mirror with wooden hand[...]
decorated with secret eye of [...]
us in black and white.
XIth Dynasty
Deir El Bahri

## LIMITED USE

Objects that lose their function turn into a relic that we no longer use, yet we still attach meanings to them: "the antique object no longer has any practical application, its role being merely to signify. (...) yet it is not a-functional, nor purely 'decorative', for it has a very specific function within the system, namely the signifying of time."
Baudrillard, Jean. Le Système des Objets. (Paris: Gallimard, 1968, 77)

# MAPPING THE WALLS

TEXT: **ISABELLE MAYAULT**
PHOTOGRAPHY: **MAARTJE ALDERS**
ILLUSTRATION: **DALILA GHODBANE**

*In November 2012, following ongoing clashes in the Tahrir -
Corniche el Nil - Qasr el Aini triangle, several walls were built
to prevent protests from spreading. Some have since been taken
down, but their rise and fall have changed the inner dynamic of the
neighbourhood.*

Walls.
Once they have been erected for a long enough time, you can
pretend they were never not there.
If you had been taught, prior to
 its sudden arrival
that one day a wall would be built at the end of your street
you would have sworn that
'a long enough time'
meant a whole generation, or at least a decade.
You realise now that it doesn't take more than ten weeks to grow
accustomed to them,
these opaque masses.

One night you heard the caterpillar. You went out on your balcony and you watched it pile up bricks at 3am. You shrugged your shoulders - walls had been built not so far away on Mohamed Mahmoud Street and they'd been attacked, eroded, dismantled. You went back to bed.

That's a thing with walls. No one holds the power to predict how long they will last and for that reason, nobody takes them seriously at first, until they're taken for granted forever. As a mother might welcome her son's new love interest with polite indifference, until they decide to marry, then all the cards are silently reshuffled.

You're aware that your street was once deprived of a wall, a state of being you like to call 'wall-less'. For once they have been built up and then taken down, there's a void.

That's another thing with walls - you can never quite go back to how it was before. The liberated space feels empty, and open, and a little bit scary. It definitely does not feel 'normal'.

Today you have to go through the corner shop, the one with two entrances, to cross the wall from entrance A to entrance B, otherwise there's a long detour.

Going through the shop is your best option to overcome the obstacle without being forced to jump over it
- which you're not very tempted to do anyway
since you know,
from experience,
that a row of tired-looking kids
wearing blue uniforms, carrying useless war weaponry
stand on the other side, in a sea of barbed wire.
Diligently, you respect the shop's opening hours. You develop the habit of walking twenty minutes, sometimes thirty,

to reach downtown.
What used to be a ten minute walk, a four guinea taxi ride,
becomes a longer walk, an eight guinea ride,
but even those facts,
irritating for the first few weeks,
have now long vanished from the conscious part of your brain.
The norm has changed,
and you have no reason to dwell.
For walls are powerful creatures, sly norm transformers.
Rulers have a thing for them.

# LEGLESS HORSE BAR

TEXT: **GABI MANGA**
PHOTOGRAPHY: **MAYADA WADNOMIRY**

*The Spy Who Loved Me* was filmed in Cairo. Despite its very liberal interpretation of distance in Egypt (Abu Simbal according to them is maybe an hour or two down the Nile from the Giza Pyramids) the film is a great relic of Egypt in the seventies. I like to think that the Virginian is where Roger Moore's (hypothetical) alcoholic stepbrother might have spent the entirety of the production process.

Located in the Moqqatam district of Cairo, the Virginian has in no way changed since the times when James Bond was gallivanting through Oum el Donya, committing lustful acts of petty espionage. Moqqatam is the location of the Zabaleen trash collectors, the Cave Church where one can still go and see live exorcisms performed, and a middle class square with the full gamut of Western fast food restaurants. And, until recently, it was also home to the headquarters of the Muslim Brotherhood, which has subsequently been destroyed.

With this schizophrenia as its backdrop, the Virginian does little to bring one back from surrealism.

Getting to Moqqatam is a majestic experience. Located on the Corniche (edge, cliffs) of the neighbourhood, one must instruct the cab driver to dodge a series of extremely zealous cafe owners/ swindlers who will gladly throw themselves in front of your car in order to serve you overpriced tea and shisha. Once you circumvent this gauntlet you are home free. You'll know you are at the Virginian when you see on your left a house that looks like it was designed by the love child of Buckminster Fuller and a freshman art student who was really into Dali.

The Virginian is loosely horse themed, horse racing in particular. Why they didn't opt for the Kentuckian isn't exactly clear, but then again this is an Egyptian locale of amusement, using logic and reason will only lead you towards migraine. Upon entering, you will be greeted by a faded picture of a horse with the bar's name over the top of it, and for some reason a picture of a bulldog with an ice pack on its head. This serves as some sort of cryptic message for the ensuing hangover you will have from drinking too much Stella. In its completely mirrored hallways the 'good time' atmosphere really starts to come into full effect with *Happy New Year 201–* written in tape on the mirrors/walls, because why take all your decorations down when you could simply change the last number of the year for a decade? Passing through this corridor you will see the indoor section of the bar and restaurant area that have not been utilised since Camp David.

You will have your *Aha!* moment, however, when you get to the terrace and realise that the Virginian is, in fact, a magical place worthy of your patronage (Note: Don't say *Aha!* out loud, as it is the colloquial term for *merde* in Egyptian Arabic). From the terrace the City Victorious spans far and wide; a breathtaking (don't breath in too hard - pollution) view of the southern reaches of Cairo and Giza.

On a clear day, not only will you see the Giza Pyramids, but also their sisters at Sakkara and Dashour further down the Nile. It is no wonder that if you frequent the Virginian enough you will inevitably become an extra in one of the TV romances that are often filmed there.

Seating along the edge of the terrace is always available, as the Virginian doesn't exactly do heavy business. Your counterparts on the terrace will usually be a series of feral cats (harmless, sometimes even cute) and occasionally a couple on a very romantic, more often than not, sober date, as the Virginian also serves juice. Accompanying you at your table will be a series of white horse statues that no longer have arms/hooves/whatever the front legs of a horse are called. I like to imagine a group of radicals stormed the Virginian only to find a bar that already looked to have been abandoned, and thus were forced to break off the legs of the horses to gain some sense of accomplishment. Little did they know they would only be adding to its dusty charm.

The music at the Virginian is excellent. They have two stereo systems: one a pseudo modern set of four-foot high subwoofers, the other a portable radio that Roger Moore's alcoholic step brother left behind. It is from the latter that the best of the music permeates the surroundings. An eclectic mix of Fairouz, Tom Jones and Sade superbly complement the scene. If you are in the mood for something in particular you are more than welcome to peruse the small sampling of cassette tapes that lie next to said radio.

Drinking often leads to hunger, but don't eat at the Virginian. The waiter with one glassy eye is a sweetheart and eager to serve, however the Virginian is home to possibly the world's worst fries. Given fries do not exactly entail the highest degree of difficulty to make, I'd caution against delving further into the menu, stick to the Teramis (Lupin Beans) and Chickpeas. Be sure to garnish them with lime.

Back to the view, truly not enough can be said about this. The only sore spot in the entire panorama is the military installation at the bottom of the Moqqatam hills, which might be the world's only military base, situated below the best vantage point from which to defend/bombard a city. Beyond this, it is incredible. Get to the Virginian at least an hour and a half before sunset. Cairo's pollution will take years off your life, but just the bad ones when you would have been be senile anyway. In the meantime the pollution produces sunsets containing a spectacular spectrum of oranges, blues and reds, with the sun itself turning from static sphere to an amorphous stream of warmth. Bring your camera, you'll look great in front of it as the sun's rays refract into a natural sepia filter that bounces off both your cheekbones and curves of the green Stella bottles.

As the sun fades, Cairo becomes a sea of lights and the view from the Virginian turns into something strikingly similar to scenes shot from the Hollywood Hills, only with a call to prayer echoing throughout the streets beneath, and youths shooting high powered green lasers into the night.

**ADDRESS:**
*CORNICHE EL MOQATTAM,*
*MOQATTAM*
*OPENING HOURS: 11AM - 2AM*

# TRAVELS THROUGH THE VITRINE

TEXT: **HEBA HABIB**

PHOTOGRAPHY: **MAARTJE ALDERS**

Once upon a time downtown shops were vast department stores run by Jews, Greeks and Cypriots with Parisian aspirations and cosmopolitan names - Sednaoui, Cicurel, Simon Arzt.

You can still find the shops. Their architecture intact, their names emblazoned in crumbling plaster.

Now they are overcrowded with mannequins with lopsided grins, bird cages, fish tanks, stuffed toys and taxidermied animals with bared fangs and paws shimmering with bracelets.

Just look a little closer.

Cairo delights in the surreal. Not in a knowing way. It just happens to be like that.

# LIBERATION CABARET

TEXT: **EBADA NAGUIB**

It was one of the strangest times of my life. I was reeling and lost after the end of a marriage that had soured and finally rotted after ten years - unsure of myself, overjoyed, terrified.

On one of those nights in the earliest days of the divorce process, I found myself at the birthday party of an equally lost friend. She too was stuck in a bad marriage and longing desperately for another man; in fact everyone at that party was a bit lost. We were all artists or working in film, a party of misfits.

We were at this swanky restaurant feeling restless until Sally - the birthday girl - suddenly announced that she had never been to a cabaret, and that it was about time she went. And a few drinks into the night this sounded like a marvellous idea, so we leapt into our cars and drove out to Haram Street - the infamous cabaret district.

We decided to go to Princess, which was owned by the very famous belly dancer and actress, Lucy. Upon arrival we were greeted by hulking bouncers who informed us that the cover charge was 350 Egyptian pounds. I was completely stunned - the poshest clubs in Cairo don't cost that much to get in. But here we were, and there was no turning away.

As suspected the whole scene resembled every single Egyptian film about cabarets I had ever seen: sweaty-browed businessmen all over the room, spangly silver décor, dizzying red, blue and green lights twisting about on the ceiling, and a heavy miasma of mingled sweetish shisha smoke and cigarettes.

We settled down at our table near the stage and were served a random mix of fruits, cheeses, nuts and mezze; bulk seeming to compensate for quality. From then on our party promptly began to drink and loosen up.

The opening act of the night was a group of women dressed in the sort of second hand clothes you buy off the pavement downtown: tight, shiny crop-tops with scatterings of cheap, holographic sequins, tiny skirts scarcely covering their bottoms and thigh-high boots with scuffed toes. Their faces were heavily plastered with makeup, their hair stiffened with spray.

They were imperfect by all standards, their large bellies spilling over the waistbands of their skirts, their thighs jiggling over the their boots, and yet as they danced to Shaabi music spun by a vicious-looking, whippet-thin DJ. As they allowed themselves to be leered at and ogled by the patrons of the cabaret, it struck me that there was nothing contrived, nothing in their expressions that was happy or sad. They smiled, laughed and writhed to the music but they were there, in that moment, deeply present in their own lives in a way we could not be. Here we were, escaping from our lives into this world, Sally to pursue the man she really wanted, the others to paw at each other or say something honest.

The women had no time for shame, they had no time to consider if they were perfect or not - they let their flesh hang out there in a way that I could never.

Intoxicated, I realised that the further down you go, you exist more truly - and there is something more powerful about people like that, more emancipated because there is no philosophy standing between you and simply being. And there is a great deal of suffering in that, but there is also suffering in thinking yourself out of life entirely - even as I recollect that moment, I know my impressions of it are marred by constant analysis. I went to the bathroom after they were done and, with some effort, caught sight of myself in the mirror. Suddenly

I realised I was present. I was not just an unseen voyeur: I was here, I was an actor in this.

After the women finished dancing they spread around the room to chit-chat with the men. I watched them entranced, one man letting his hand slide up the thigh of a girl.

The second act was a proper belly dancer in a traditional tight galabeya and a coquettishly tied headscarf. She was incredibly sexy but you could tell every move was calculated to be so. Every swivel of her hip, every shimmy was choreographed and it stood in stark contrast with the girls that were dancing before.

She was wonderful to watch, clacking her castanets and winking at the crowd, up until one of our party found the nerve to get up on stage.

The final act of the night was Lucy, the cabaret owner herself. As soon as she entered, the place was electrified; she was amazing to behold.

She chitchatted with the crowd, roused them to dance as she herself began to sway and swish across the stage, then suddenly vanishing and returning in a totally new outfit, again and again, all of them tight, provocative and blazing with colour.

Still, despite her showmanship, somehow everyone was acting in a strangely scripted way, as if this entire scene was snipped from a film, that would have been pasted frame by frame onto reality itself.

We left soon after Lucy's act, but I've never forgotten that evening. I still think about it every now and again and about those women who revealed such unnerving truths about me, something that ripped through the smoke, the loud music, the lechery and the floors made slippery with spilt beer.

*Nights at the cabaret are a serious affair: Dress boldly, act shamelessly, and don't drink too heavily.*

*For a less costly cabaret experience we recommend the Scheherazade in Alfy Street downtown, but the true blue deal is the infamous Haram Street in Giza. Proceed with caution and expect anything.*

# A THOUSAND NIGHTS
# AT LEILAS

TEXT: **ISABELLE MAYAULT**

PHOTOGRAPHY: **MAGALI COROUGE**

"Is Leila coming?" I ask. It's one of those dry summer evenings. We're seated on dusty mattresses, on a rooftop lit up like the front deck of a boat. Garden City lies below, quiet and dark.

"You mean Leila Mourad?" asks one of the tenants, laughing. "I'd be surprised if she showed up," says my host, "Leila died in the nineties."

That night, I'm told that the former owner of the place is not, contrary to what I had assumed, one of those twenty-something activists who fill up curfew parties. Rather, Leila Mourad used to be one of Egypt's most renowned singers and actresses. She was sacred, the 'official singer of the Revolution' in 1953. She even beat Oum Kalthum to it, although Oum is rumoured to have been Nasser's favorite.

Leila has been gone for decades, but taxi drivers still know her address by heart. All you have to say is 'Beet Leila Mourad' (Leila Mourad's house) and they'll drop you in front of the door, down a leafy street, a few yards away from the Nile.

"There's more," my host continues "Leila Mourad's husband bet, and lost, their apartment when playing cards with a friend on this very rooftop." She pauses and points to the floor. "They lost it just like that," she says, snapping her fingers in the hot air.

Suddenly, I see us as intruders, squatters, young Leninists occupying the former reception hall of a royal family forced into exile.

How did Leila's husband break the news to her? Did she attend the fatal card game? Did she start drinking afterwards? Where did she spend the last years of her life?

"What would she think if she could see us chatting on her roof, like we belong here?"

"Maybe she does see us," someone says.

Seven people live at Leila's and even though some settled here more than a year ago, they haven't all met each other. They're unsure of who's left and who hasn't. "It's a bit like living in a train station," says Anja, who had a fever that night.

Two corridors converge to the living room. You can hear people walking on the creaking floorboards.

The living room can be a little intimidating. Someone will always be there, sitting in one of the extravagant armchairs, and you might think some performance is about to be delivered to them or to the entire neighbourhood.

Because of the soft, fresh autumn breeze running at all times through the French windows, but also because of the way residents peacefully greet each other, smoke and read all day, hanging out at Leila's feels a little bit like spending the afternoon on a Scandinavian beach during summertime (for it is now November in Cairo, and only in November can you be tempted to compare its climate to the hottest months in Copenhagen or Oslo).

At first, you might mistake the apartment as one that is not quite taken care of, the floors are dirty and the furniture odd. But then you begin to notice things, sheets neatly piled up in one of the main room's cupboards, fridges filled with fruits and lentil-based dishes, utensils hung in both kitchens that are diverse and sophisticated, the kind that only serious cooks bother to pack.

All you have to do is go there and lie down on one of the rusty mattresses and you will hear the world come to you in small waves. If you're lucky, the deck will be moon lit and all of the disappointments of Cairo will vanish in the silver light.

But it might as well go the other way around. It looks like one of those dramatic settings where fatal conversations occur - small treasons, big break-ups, unforgiveable card games. As if Leila, in her mighty absence, was holding the cards forever deciding, according to her whim, to save or damn you.

# AN ESCAPIST'S PLAYGROUND

## SEARCHING FOR AN IDEAL APARTMENT DOWNTOWN

TEXT: **HANDE YANIZOGLU**

PHOTOGRAPHY: **IASON ATHANASIADIS**

The first thing I notice about the approaching *simsara* (real estate broker): the lines etched by her long black dress in the district's sandy streets. Her face radiates an insolent pessimism. More prison warden than polished real estate agent, she arrives on the scene after being summoned by a neighbourhood tough called Ahmad, who chases after us into the staircase of an expansively derelict building off Maruf Street that we've tried to explore. For a few brief minutes - until Ahmad shatters our bubble - the stairway's broken, Egyptian-blue windows, carved, wooden doors and graceful spiral railings become our escapist playground.

This is one of the many half-abandoned buildings in downtown Cairo, harking back to the city's *belle époque*, now left to rot gently. Many are remnants of the era that began with the rule of Khedive Ismail, Egypt's late nineteenth century, Paris-educated moderniser,

who ordered the replacement of Cairo's busy districts with Parisian-style wide boulevards and orderly grids.

As most of the residents inhabiting these areas fled Egypt in the first half of the century and Cairo's bourgeois neighbourhoods expanded to areas like Dokki, Ma'adi and Mohandiseen, today's downtown stands as a decaying open-air museum; a collection of run-down buildings, either entirely empty or used as offices, with ground floors featuring fluorescently-lit toy stores, dusty-shelved pharmacies, and local fast-food joints. The buildings are decomposing due to neglect and a lack of resources for the preservation of architectural heritage. Often, age is used as an excuse to demolish and build 'modern'.

At the turn of the century, this now overlooked corner of downtown, with its dusty streets and poor residents congregated in shabby cafes, had been one of Cairo's chicest districts. Neoclassical buildings that featured high ceilings, nostalgic window shutters and elegant wooden floors arose from hastily cleared shantytowns. On this morning, we have set out on a walk, counting on our luck as we inquire in coffee shops and corner kiosks in the hope that we might stumble upon such an apartment.

Ahmed exchanges a few whispers with the *simsara*, likely agreeing to a share of profits if I settle in one of the flats she will show me. She finally leads us away, with her old cell phone stuck between her ear and headscarf. As we enter the first building, she is confronted by its *bawab*, an unavoidable character in the life of many apartment-residents in the city. The *bawab* can roughly be defined as the caretaker of a building with functions including market- delivery, light bulb-changing and intelligence-collection, but more symbolically, he manifests the building's character. Most come from Upper Egypt and inhabit an over-crowded room with their large families, by the entrance. On ads for flats catering to foreigners, one frequently finds a note about their characteristics, ranging from

'super-friendly', 'slightly moody' to 'discreet'.

The *bawab* is the newcomer's first encounter with this culture of delicate intrusion. One soon notices that he keeps an excruciatingly accurate tab on the inhabitant's times of departure and return, and can throw a truly scornful glance after a night of unknown guests.

This building's *bawab* is a corpulent, middle-aged man, sporting a bulky *galabiyya* and cap ensemble of the same maize hue. Marking his territory, he leaves the *simsara* at the entrance, leading us upstairs in an elevator decorated with hand-written revolutionary slogans. As we make our way down through a filthy, narrow corridor lit by fluorescent lights, door signs give away clues about the other occupants: a doctor, a tailor, an insurance office.

The flat features a rusty kitchen with a yellowing sink, a stridently buzzing 1970s refrigerator, two couches with ragged, velvety covers, and carpets bearing marks of intense livelihood. The *simsara* finally barges in after a few minutes, casting suspicious glances at us: "What do you think?" she asks, a challenging look in her eyes. We demur politely. After two further attempts she leaves us on the pavement, cursing us for refusing to compensate her for the showings.

The more we search, the more it became apparent that downtown's fine apartments rarely go on the market, or fall in the hands of greedy *simsars*. A tribal network of acquaintances and families who share a common appreciation of the city's heritage, trust each other with their properties and jealously guard them. One acquaintance had inherited a beautiful villa built in the 1920s by his family in Garden City; another was passed on a light-filled flat with burgundy walls through diplomatic connections.

How could the newcomer find points of entry into this invisible network? Would it take years, gradual integration, or pure chance?

In my case it was partly the latter. I met the owner of my flat on a downtown street as I walked with a friend whose family had lived in downtown for generations. A friend of his, she was getting ready with her partner to dance the curfew away to live music. Like the buildings surrounding her, she appeared to belong to a bygone era: blonde curls unevenly cut; a classic, cream dress; perfect French and German.

"You're looking for a flat?" she said, waving hands whose nails had been chipped away by the work she had put into several weeks of renovations. "I've just finished mine on Qasr al-Aini. Would you like to see it?"

Qasr al-Aini is one of the major arteries of downtown Cairo. After 2011, it became a playground for revolutionaries, with open-ended sit-ins and spray cans unleashing revolutionary creativity on the district's walls. Eventually, the army constructed two large walls to block off access to Tahrir, creating labyrinths of concrete for those trying to navigate the area.

Trying to reach the flat, I found that the only option for getting through the wall running the width of the street, was to go through a corner supermarket, whose second door opened on the other side of the wall. Up the creaky elevator and there I was - a beautiful flat with every detail embodying the owner's Cairene soul; shelved books on the city's architectural heritage, old Egyptian films on VHS, Mameluke-era table lamps, her grandmother's porcelain plates. It stole my heart. As I watched her offering the foreman of the repair crew a glass of wine for his troubles, I decided that - alongside the ideal apartment - I might have found the perfect landlord.

A few days after I moved in, we shared drinks at a downtown bar.

"You awakened a feeling of trust in me when I first met you," she said as we nibbled on *sujuk* and cheese samosas.

We talked about the revolution, Cairo's theatre scene, Germany in the eighties, Istanbul's summer protests. We agreed to go dancing when she got back from a two-month trip. At that moment, I knew I would live her house and Cairo the way she lived it - I would keep its soul intact. And that's probably the best hint one can give to those looking to land one of the gems of downtown Cairo.

RECREATE

# BURSA NIGHTS

TEXT: **AHMED HEGAB**

PHOTOGRAPHY: **MAGALI COROUGE**

Everyone will tell you that Tahrir Square is the most important part of downtown, and though I would rather not go where so many have gone before, it is doubtless where downtown Cairo begins.

The best time to really observe and walk around downtown is on Friday mornings at 8am or on Saturdays at a similar hour. This is when most of the government offices are closed and when there are no crowds, so you can saunter around in the sunshine and truly take in its loveliness. It's like observing a great actress alone in her boudoir, her hair loose and her face without makeup, looking surprisingly youthful despite her advanced years.

This doesn't mean I don't like visiting downtown at night. In fact for the last fifteen years this is where I like to be the most, even though the cafes, especially in the Bursa area, have become incredibly crowded over the three years following the Revolution. Finding myself in the midst of the hubbub of a thousand conversations and the mingled scents from hundreds of shishas with their fruit-flavoured tobacco makes me feel like part of the eternal noise of Cairo.

Downtown is not simply the centre of the capital but the centre of all of Egypt, and of its history too. You can sense it - sense the Egyptian and English soldiers stomping through at the beginning of the twentieth century, sense the archers and cavalrymen train as

they did three hundreds years ago, see Napoleon's generals strolling through on their way to their headquarters that were located downtown. They are all there - just obscured by time.

The way downtown looks now can be dated to when the tram system was installed in Ataba, Azbakia and Shubra in 1903. In a way it has been the same piano since then but with different keys, some from one hundred and eighty years ago, some from one hundred years ago and some from a mere twenty - this is very typical of Cairo, but is at its most charming downtown, to my eye.

The building that looks like it shouldn't be at all present downtown is the AUC library building in Mohamed Mahmoud Street - an odious block of cement with pretensions to modernism - but even that has harmoniously fused with the rest of downtown after it was used as a canvas for graffiti artists. Leaving Tahrir Square and entering Talaat Harb, I get a strange pleasure from merely passing by Café Riche - I have never entered the place but to see its painted glass front and dark green awning is strangely reassuring. This was the place where Egypt's greatest intellectuals met and where Naguib Mahfouz would hold his weekly salon; it is also where young artists and novelists from all over the Arab world came to be introduced to this unparalleled Egyptian genius. I still wonder why I have never actually gone in. Perhaps I am waiting for the right moment to sit inside and bask in the glow of that glorious past.

Whenever I set a date to meet someone downtown I like to meet in front of the Shorouk bookstore because the pavement is wider there and it is always a pleasure to let your eye roam over the Art Deco architecture of the square - and if whoever I am meeting is a little late, I like to cross to the other side and stand before the famous Salon De Groppi to admire the architecture from that side. This is something I never tire of, and it is always a great deal of fun to imagine all the beautiful young people that used to frequent Groppi in the days when there was a permanent band there, whiskey was served and King Farouk saw fit to send a basket full of their goodies to the young princesses Margaret and Elizabeth. Still now their *fruits glacés* are delectable.

It's also amusing to observe the rowdy clothes and accessory sellers dotted all over the square, yelling to advertise their products to a largely indifferent public. A lot of people complain about these vendors, saying they have defaced downtown and made it intolerable, but to me they are an essential element in what makes downtown such an exceptional place. It has din, silence, the grace of aged buildings, the ferocity of angry youthful graffiti, elegance, squalour, charming bohemian artists all in one area!

Another stopping point near Talaat Harb is the infamous Felfela restaurant - where all tourists must go just for its timeless charm and excellent Egyptian food - it's a little like dining in an Arcadian grotto complete with chirping birds, fish tanks and painted glass ceiling with vines hanging overhead.

Another of my favourite downtown haunts is the Hawamedya market cafe in Bab el Louk - El Hamdeya is a famous Syrian market - the cafe was originally opened by a Syrian in 1960 as an ice cream and pastry shop directly after Syria and Egypt were declared one country - the United Arab Republic. The cafe is the last remaining symbol of the unification of Syria and Egypt - despite the fact that the union only lasted three years.

The first thing that will catch your attention is the cafe owner's moustache - an Egyptian Syrian called Talal el Nahas - a carefully waxed levantine monster of a moustache - the aura of which overwhelms the place. The cafe had its golden age in the 1980s but is still worth visiting just to rub shoulders with the young independent thinkers and artists of downtown - and to see that moustache of course - a relic worthy of going on a pilgrimage.

The Souk el Hamdeya cafe is on a pavement between Falaki Street and Abd el Salam Aref Street. Beside it on Falaki Street you will find the Nadwa il Thaqafeya cafe (the cultural debate cafe) despite or perhaps because of its pompous sounding name, this is one of the most famous cafes downtown - especially famous for serving *Tinbak* - a luxurious kind of *Ma'3asel* shisha tobacco (*Ma'3asel* is tobacco that has been stewed in honey). It's also very famous for being another meeting point for the city's intelligentsia and independent musicians. The bands Wust el Balad and Black Theama are known to frequent Nadwa very often.

On the right of the Hamdeya Market cafe is the Bon Abd el Ma'boud coffee mill, which in my opinion sells the best coffee in Cairo - I can never pass by without buying an eighth of a kilo of light coffee, flavoured with dried roses. I always buy small amounts so I can go in often to enjoy the sight of the old coffee mills grinding away, and the smell of fresh beans being pounded into powder.

No day in downtown is complete without stopping off at the infamous Horreya Cafe - an eighty year old cafe and one of the few to still sell Stella beer. Watch out for the head waiter Milad though - you will discover why for yourself.

# I AM NOT MY NAME

TEXT: **KHAIRY BESHARA** AS TOLD TO **ROBERT BESHARA**

My name is Khairy Beshara, at least that is the name I was given at birth on June 30, 1947 in the city of Tanta, Egypt. Obviously, I am not my name.

As I was becoming famous as a filmmaker, around the time when I had received many awards for my second documentary film, *The Village Doctor* (1975), my birth name started turning into a celebrity name. As someone who likes to challenge labels, categories and definitions (in the Nietzschean sense), I started feeling distant from my name - which by 1990 had become a social commodity, particularly with the box office success of my film *Crab*, which happens to be from my own filmography, one of my favorite films, the other being being *Sweet Day, Bitter Day* (1988). Fame was alienating to me because I did not make films to get awards or to be recognised, I made films because I took it as my duty to change the social reality in Egypt. My work was kind of like the Cinema of the Oppressed to borrow from Augusto Boal.

My family and I moved to Cairo when I was six years old, to Shubra, but I still have fond memories of my childhood in Sidi Salem. My dad used to work for this British company before Gamal Abdel Nasser nationalised it, and so we lived in this rural town that felt like the English countryside. We had a two-storey house with a

front yard and all. The scenes from my recollections during those formative years informed my aesthetic sensibility as a filmmaker or so I found out years later: the sunsets, the trees, the butterflies... they were all rich in colours. The closest I came to translating these amorphous visuals into film language was through the following 'critically acclaimed' projects: The *Collar and the Bracelet* (1986) and *Sweet Day, Bitter Day* (1988). I like to say that the *mise-en-scène* in my documentaries has the aesthetic of a fiction film, and that my narrative films have the spirit of a documentary film.

My uncle Kamel Fahmy had a huge influence on me. I found his personality to be quite unique. One day, I came across his English briefcase, and I opened it as a young adolescent - probably I was twelve years of age - as if it were a treasure chest, and lo and behold, I was charmed by what I found: books! My uncle worked in theatre and radio, which inspired me to get into theatre. My dream was to become an actor - the myth is that it is the repressed dream of all film directors. I did not really pursue that, except through the occasional cameos in Mohamed Khan's films. My best friend tells me I bring him good luck, but I think he is just biased because he likes me.

What I loved about Shubra was the active social life, the beautiful chaos: neighbours talking to one another through their windows, produce sellers hollering the names of their vegetables, and people walking on the street all day long. After moving to Nasr City, I was unable to call the grocer from the balcony, so I miss the warmth and spontaneity of social interactions in Shubra. And of course, I miss the old basket with a rope trick, the Egyptian equivalent of a dumb waiter.

When I was a student at the Higher Cinema Institute (HCI), the Dean was Hassan Fahmy, a man ahead of his time. Fahmy revolutionised education at the HCI by introducing a number of courses unrelated to film but that were important for his film students to have a sense of general knowledge. For example, we took science courses, and a course on etiquette to name a few. He also introduced the concept of a full day (i.e finishing school in the evening) because before him we were done in the early afternoon. His daughter, Farida Kamel, was responsible for having folkloric dance be taken seriously as an academic subject.

Here is an interesting story: Hassan saw Elia Kazan one day on the street in downtown during the summer. We (the students) were on break at that point. Hassan invited Kazan to the HCI, and to my good luck I was present and met the legendary American filmmaker. Some other students were there, too. This was probably around 1964-1965; I was seventeen at the time. I had mixed feelings about meeting Kazan because I was a fan of two of his films: *A Streetcar Named Desire* (1951) and *America, America* (1963), but at the same time I disliked his duplicitous role during the McCarthy era.

After graduating from the HCI in 1967, I went to Poland - where I met my wife - for two years as part of a fellowship. When I returned to Egypt, I felt like a stranger in a strange land. I knew more about Poland than I did about Egypt, so I decided to discover my country through the lens of documentary filmmaking.

Right now, I have a complicated relationship with Cairo. Al Qahera - the transliteration of the Arabic word - means 'the defeater.' Growing up in Shobra from 1953 till 1992, a neighbourhood that was marked by diversity: Christians and Muslims living side by side, I witnessed the cultural decline of Egypt starting with Anwar Sadat's 'openness' policy and ending with Hosni Mubarak's corrupt police state, the consequences of which the country is still recovering from.

When I want to renew my relationship with the city, I go to Café Riche. It contains my memories with my wife when we came back from Poland in the early 1970s. I made many friends there: writers, composers, etc. I love seeing Filfil and Magdy. Filfil has been working there since before I was born, and Magdy - he's just a lover of books. Riche was where the intelligentsia gathered. It reminds me of Egypt's

golden era, and my personal history: how I became who I am, how I developed my own consciousness, and what I love about Egypt. It is a fountain of memories. The photographs on the walls are of the leaders of the Egyptian Enlightenment in modern Egypt. Riche is a symbol of leftism, the sixties generation, and revolutionary angst. My favourite memories are from the time spent there in the years of culture and rebellion.

For me, modern Egypt can be summarised in Café Riche, which was founded in 1908. Two centuries, one café. Naguib Mahfouz, one of the people I used to hang out with there, wrote a novel called *Karnak Café*. It is about Riche.

Today, Riche is fighting for survival. If Riche closes down one day, that will signal the death of the true spirit of modern Egypt. If Riche closes down my relationship with Cairo will become even more complicated.

My favourite two Egyptian actresses I worked with are Sherihan and Faten Hamam (Omar el Sherif's ex-wife). What impressed me about Sherihan was her intelligence, instinct, enormous energy and spontaneity. She almost seemed to read my thoughts!

I was not aware of Faten Hamam's stature until after I finished *Sweet Day, Bitter Day* (1988), which could have been her one hundreth film. After all, she was one of my childhood heroines, but I tried to not let that distract me. We had an excellent working relationship marked by mutual trust. She adored *The Collar and The Bracelet* (1986), and one time she asked me: "what can we work on?" I had two film ideas: one concerning an Egyptian immigrant who returns from the USA, and the other related to a Shubra study. She then asked: "what is close to your heart?" I responded: "Shubra!" Then she said: "since the film will be about Shubra, I will not be the leading actress, but I still want to do it." This is really what dreams are made of, my story with Faten Hamam feels like a fairy tale at this point. When I became angry on the set due to exhaustion, impatience or disappointment, she was very supportive. She used to come next to me and in a caring voice would say: "go on, I am with you." She is a pure soul... I used to call her Tuna or Aisha, but never Faten or Madame Faten. She showed me where she used to live in Shubra as a child. Ultimately, she was happy with the experiment even though it was challenging for her because it was her return to a distant place, a sweet memory.

The filmmaker who best captured Cairo on film: Mohamed Khan. Do you know the story of the Cleansing of the Temple? This is from the New Testament, wherein Jesus expels the moneychangers from the Temple, accusing them of turning the Temple into a den of thieves through their commercial activities. Replace the Temple with Cairo, and you will understand the cultural decline from the sacred to the profane, starting all the way back to Ancient Egypt. We (Egyptian filmmakers) have so much history, and so much to tell, we have not even begun. In Western cinema, they have almost run out of ideas. We, on the contrary, are full of potential, but we are burdened by our history, by our past, and because of that we freeze in the present. What does it mean to be an Egyptian today? How do we envision our new identities? Please, recall that I am not my name.

# THOSE RADIO DAYS

## PLAYING WITH OUM KALTHOUM

TEXT: **HUSSEIN ELSHAFIE**

PHOTOGRAPHY: **NURAH FARAHAT**

"Those radio days, before I even became a musician - every first Thursday of the month, we used to buy *marrons*, light the gas grill and listen to Oum Kalthoum's monthly concert. This ritual went on for decades."

Books, photographs, postcards, musical instruments and gramophones are piled up on the shelves. An old, small TV, positioned at an awkward angle so that one can barely notice it, and an enormous, wooden desk that has long lost all its features, behind which sits Samir, a music shop owner and flutist, once also a well-known figure on the Egyptian music scene in the second half of the twentieth century.

"She used to love her band profoundly," he continues "her accordionist, Farouk Salama, would only perform solos during the concert without joining the ensemble, and before each concert she would be sure to invite him. He was also the youngest band member. His talent was surreal."

L'Amour Éternel

"Both her zitherist and violinist, Abdo Saleh and Ahmed Elhefnawy respectively, used to receive a deafening applause whenever either of them performed a solo during one of her concerts. Audiences used to relish in instrumental music. They did not go to concerts to only watch Oum Kalthoum. They went to watch her and her band."

"Whenever one of her band members died, she would keep their chair empty in commemoration during rehearsals and concerts. She also had a chair. She used to sit on it during the orchestral intro."

"I had one black tuxedo. Before each concert or gala, I used to have it dry cleaned and then iron it..." He pauses. I notice the voice of Halim, breaking faintly from the old TV on the counter: *any sad tear no no no no. Any wounded heart no no no no...*

The music continues, Halim continues. In that remarkably long moment of relative silence, I can see Samir's indifferent eyes sparkle, his whole apathetic composure becomes one of attentiveness and pride.

"Sometimes there are handymen renovating the shop, and he'll yell at them. Then, when he hears a song on TV, he stops yelling. He even forgets what he's yelling about," Samir's assistant whispers to me. "In the old days, whenever musicians liked a piece, they would listen to each other's recital of it, and with their own instrument, get inspired and compete to master it. Since DJs started, this activity has died out. Now with the tap of a button you can play violin, oud or zither. All levels of complication, originality and ingenuity are gone."

"Whenever I listen to a piece of music from the old days, I see our world as beautiful," Samir picks up the conversation "music creates beauty in any place it seeps into. It beautifies it. There is a tremendous difference between the experience of watching a live concert and listening to it on the radio. Theatre is so picturesque. You can see each musician while listening to them play."

"Halim's musical background made him both the vocalist and the conductor of the Diamond Band. He used to introduce them one by one to the audience before each concert started. He once even interrupted a concert to apologetically introduce Samir Surour, his saxophonist, whom he had forgotten to introduce."

"He used to buy us kebabs for dinner, then sit down and eat half a plate of pudding and a handful of tablets. His weak liver could not be accustomed to food. It was painful seeing such a beautiful artist taking tablets."

"The difference between the old and the new in Egyptian music rhetoric is a difference of timelessness. We knew that once a piece of music had been recorded, it lived. And we wouldn't have recorded it hadn't we loved it. During our rehearsals, we used to do sight-reading in the first few sessions only, until we had ingested it and blended with it. Then, during final rehearsals, we would not read the music. We would live it."

# THE YOUNG LADY REVOLTS

TEXT: LEILA ISKANDAR

Heliopolis, the most perfect suburb of Cairo, is where I was born in the year of our Lord 1942. It seems like so long ago, but I remember it all vividly.

The Heliopolis I grew up in was like a vast playground - its landmarks ruled our lives, and when I say we, I mean my group of friends. Seventeen, eighteen and nineteen year-old boys and girls who mostly went to French schools (one or two went to English schools).

Our school was a beautiful Art Deco building on Beirut Street, with pure architectural lines and lush gardens. The Sacré Cœur, Heliopolis, is where I received my thorough and demanding education administered by solemn, strict nuns. Of course, as unruly girls, we resented their toughness but now I cherish the discipline they gave me.

On Sundays, our meeting point was the Basilic Church. After Mass, we would all set off to the Heliopolis sporting club for lunch. I still go there to this day. It stands behind what was Cairo's most sumptuous hotel, which later became the presidential palace.

This is where my parents got married and later also one of my youngest aunts. The famous Oum Kulthum was singing at her wedding. She pulled at her handkerchief in a melodramatic way, like in all poignant moments, when I started to imitate her, thinking it was irresistibly funny. My parents were forced to lock me up in a cloakroom so I wouldn't cause a scandal - I was only five or six at the time but it wasn't the last time my sense of humour landed me in hot water!

Back to our Sundays: one of our favourite pastimes was racing our cars to the Pyramids. It only took around twenty minutes back then, as there was little traffic and wonderfully smooth roads, not to mention that we were all a little crazy.

We rode horses, had breakfast at the Mena House Hotel, which was majestic and terribly chic.

Downtown Cairo was for movies - Metro, Radio or Rivoli - then sandwiches at Bamboo. We rarely went to restaurants. It was not really our thing. We were more into dancing, potluck parties or strolling in the streets of Cairo.

Dancing was mainly the thing - we were all mad about it. We would go dancing at Stereo at the Pyramids, the Airport discotheque, the Merryland nightclub or After Eight downtown. We also danced at the houses of friends, whose parents were open-minded enough to let them throw parties (I met my husband at one of those parties).

Sometimes we also loved to go to Sahara city, a city of chalets behind the pyramids. It was especially lovely on moonlit nights, and romantic of course.

When we were broke, we went to La Grenouille, a small nightclub where we used to have dancing competitions - I was a rock and roll star back then, and often won.

Now onto more serious matters. My generation was perhaps the second where women began to really enter the workplace. Very few of my mother's friends worked. Some as teachers or translators, there

149

was one writer and a photographer, but these were the elite, with no husband or kids to cramp their style - and they were exceptions.

A lot of my friends started working straight out of school, to help forward their education, others got married quickly. It was the expected thing, the proper thing to do. At the time, girls were supposed to get married early and be less of a burden and a worry to their long-suffering parents.

A girl's reputation was safe when she married young. A boy from a respectable family that the parents knew (always a plus) and if the girl wanted to work it was ok only until her parents found the proper husband for her.

On my mother's side of the family, we were nineteen cousins. Boys and girls, and maybe only two of these followed 'the marriage pattern'. As for me I had been dating for seven years when I married the man I love - a Syrian by birth, not a Coptic. The rest of the family followed suit, so for my grandfather, a Coptic patriarch, this was a shock: only four of his grandchildren married Copts. We rather broke the tradition in that way.

I studied Sociology and Anthropology at the AUC, and spent a wonderful few years making new friends and discovering new haunts: lunches at the Ibis Café at the beginning of the month, with our pockets still freshly lined with money, or at the Night & Day cafeteria at the Semiramis Hotel.

Once the studies were over, it was time to find a job. At that time, you could expect a secretarial job or a teaching job at best if you had it in you. So off girls went to study typing and stenography at 'Chez Mr Robert' to become an executive secretary, a very sought after position.

I couldn't manage. I tried three times but my fingers were too stiff and honestly, I hated the idea of being shackled to a desk job and the whims of a haughty boss. I was a rock and roll star after all! I ended up studying German at night school, which was great fun because I

went with my boyfriend - a great deal more fun than dreary typing!
I'll never forget those days of sleek girls in chic mini dresses, debonair men in trim suits and mocking smiles, with dreams growing bigger with every passing day. When everything was possible and Cairo seemed vast and free. Days gone but never forgotten.

# AN ENDLESS SUPPLY OF SUNSHINE AND PINK GIN

TEXT: **MOHAMED HABIB** AS TOLD TO **HEBA HABIB**

Gezira Club for me has been the centre of my life in Cairo - it is home in a way few places have been home to me. I remember my very first time there, I was nine years old and I had just come back from Copenhagen where my father was working as a diplomat at the Egyptian embassy. Cairo for me back then was a dimly recollected memory, but on entering the Gezira Club I was dazzled.

Endless fields of green, swings, waiters in crimson waistcoats and spotless galabeyas - so many places to play beneath an Egyptian sun that never seemed to dim. There were parks in Copenhagen of course but this idea that one could have warm, green grass and endless supply of sunshine combined was a revelatory. I haven't quite gotten over it I guess.

The club is everything you could possibly want in one place - you can play any kind of sport you can imagine, you can have wonderful meals, meet a friend for coffee. Once upon a time the club even had a bar! One of the best stocked bars in the country in fact, with terribly debonair barmen that seemed like throwbacks from when the club was the English Officers Club - I remember especially those famous Pink Gins.

Alas, the Ministry of Youth and Sport shut down the club bar in the early eighties, after an incident where a member got completely smashed and yelled at an old man who collapsed and died.

All the great memories of my childhood and youth happened here - my father, God rest his soul, would bring me here daily for karate and swimming training, and then go off to play squash and drink coffee with his friends. He was rather infamous in the club for his gentlemanly ways and ribald jokes, and I like to think I will be remembered for the same things.

I will confess that I spent most of my youth in the club getting into all sorts of trouble: I was one of the first guys in Egypt to really get into bodybuilding, along with my buddies, so we were always being called in to fight for other sports teams or over girls. I remember fighting a lot with the boys who played for the croquet team, who we all thought were very stuck up - and whenever the Heliopolis club water polo team came in to play, our water polo team would call us in to trounce the Heliopolis boys - we were all full of crazy animal energy back then.

One of my favourite memories with the boys at the gym was when what eventually became the WWF came to give a show at the club, and these muscled men in leotards and crazy masks came into the gym to train. One of my best friends at the time, Mohamed Ashoush, a real tough nut, challenged these guys to a weightlifting competition. They were tying for a while but then Ashoush proposed they bench press something like one hundred and fifty kilos and they chickened out. I'll never forget his face smiling through three litres of sweat. We couldn't stop laughing about it for weeks.

Another great thing about the club in the seventies and eighties was that the best events always happened there. I saw Julio Iglesias and Dalida in concert and perhaps even Demis Roussos.

That may not be the case so much now but I still like to go everyday if I can manage it, to take in the air, exercise and enjoy the people. The regulars, as you can imagine, are all a bit on the eccentric side, old ladies in staunch denial of their real ages, tanning in fluorescent bikinis, former karate champions gone to seed conversing with German shepherds, actors, singers, old movie producers with nothing better to do than ogle the young girls by the Lido. There's never any lack of things to talk about, whether past or present, while munching on the club's famous Escalope Maison, washed down with lemonade and mint.

Gezira Club people are my kind of people - I won't be apologetic about that - I do like people with style and Gezira Club people are largely that, especially the regulars like me who come to enjoy the beautiful surroundings, the stately oaks and elms that are some of Cairo's oldest trees - the special Gezira Club crows that nest in the tea garden trees and the bright, green lovebirds that come in Spring - the club is a small city of its own, and I have always felt like one of the princes of that city.

*To enjoy a day at the Gezira Club - pick an especially sunny day in Cairo (no lack of those but there is always that perfect one) pack your swimsuit, a thermos full of Mimosa and your fanciest sunglasses - befriend a member or sneak in by the horse stables - go directly to the Lido and don't forget to order the Escalope Maison.*

# BEIT EL 3UD

TEXT: **OLIVIA STERLING**

ILLUSTRATION: **DALILA GHODBANE**

Every Monday, Wednesday and Saturday, I get out of the taxi
shortly before Hussein Square, in Islamic Cairo. With my saz
swinging from my back, I make way through the busy side roads
surrounding the El Azhar Mosque, passing by fruit and vegetable
stands, I salute the chicken store's owner, I decline, at least three
times to start playing my instrument in the middle of the street
and I avoid several bikes, cars and donkeys. Finally, I manage
to slip through to the square known as Zainab el Khaitoun. As
always, groups of youngsters drink tea and smoke sheesha while
Mohamed Mounir's most famous tunes play inside the coffee shop.
On the Square's walls are glued pictures of Ustaz Naseer Shamma, a
renowned Iraqi oud player, along with Gamal Abdel Nasser's, Anouar
al Sadate's and, more recently, the general Sisi's portraits. Those
curious enough will walk the ten extra steps necessary to discover the
entrance of the school Naseer Shamma founded in 1998, tucked in a
corner across the square: *beet el 3ud*, also known as the house of the
Arabic Lute.

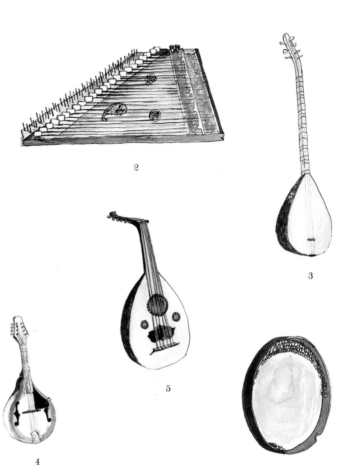

1
2
3
4
5
6

| 1. Ney | ١ الناي |
| 2. Qanun | ٢ القانون |
| 3. Saz | ٣ الصاز |
| 4. Mandoline | ٤ المندولينة |
| 5. Oud | ٥ العود |
| 6. Daff | ٦ الضاف |

0    10          50              100            150

centimeters

A few months ago, a German friend of mine, Alexandre, whose spouse is Egyptian, invited me for a cup of coffee at Zaineb el Khaitoun. He praised the beauty of the place, described to me its relaxing atmosphere, the trees hanging over the tiny, low tables, cushions littered on the floor. Then he offered to take me to have a quick look at the music school where he had been learning to play the oud for weeks, anticipating that I would enjoy visiting one of those ancient houses built in the eighteenth century. I was immediately carried away by the musical aura and the quietness of the place, and decided on the spot to start classes the following Monday.

Even after months spent in *beet el 3ud*, my first impression has not faltered. When you enter the school yard - which, as a tourist, you'll only be allowed to do during the day, evenings being reserved for the school students - you instantly forget about the fuss and the honking noises and the street vendors of the El Azhar neighbourhood. After a few steps inside, you can hear the melody of oud and saz from the yard.

Evenings at *beet el 3ud* always start with a round of saluting, which consists of traveling from one room to another - a dozen rooms in total, scattered on three different floors. Each time someone enters, the class is briefly interrupted, hands are shaken and the latest news briefly shared. If you're serious about studying at beet el 3ud, the number one rule is to have the patience to share your time with others. There are no fixed hours, no assigned classroom, no note taking. Classes occur between 4pm and 10pm. First arrived first served - students have to listen to the others while waiting for their one-to-one class with the teacher.

Meanwhile, I chat with Jawa the Syrian, Youssef the Iraqi, Nouf the Saudi and Tarek the Egyptian. Artists, high school students, lawyers, architects, professional music players, all of us range from ages ten to seventy-seven. The forty of us come from a dozen different countries. Ustaz Naseer calls us 'the big family of *beet el 3ud*'. If some are here to study music as a hobby, others pursue more serious ambitions and hope to graduate from the school, in order to start a career as promising as their master's. Mohamed Abozekry is one of them, at fifteen, he became the youngest oud professor in Egypt. He had started four years earlier as Naseer Shamma's protégé.

Naseer Shamma was born in 1963 in Kut (Iraq) where he began to play music at the age of twelve. A few years later, he graduated from the Baghdad conservatory. A composer and a writer, he has become renowned worldwide as a master of classical Arab music. After he played and taught the oud in several countries, he founded *beet el 3ud* in Cairo, where he aimed at training a new generation of musicians and professors. In order to do this, he settled in *beet el Harrawy*, one of the three houses connected to the Al Azhar Mosque.

Where could my teacher be hiding today? Depending on his mood, he will choose one room or another, sometimes on the first floor, in the shade of moucharaby, or in a remote room on the second floor, where nothing will interrupt the lesson, except maybe for the voice of the muezzin, coming from the nearby minaret of El Azhar.

When we are honoured with Ustaz Naseer's visit, students gather in the yard where they form a circle. It's time for *prova*, a collective musical session that Ustaz Naseer leads from the stage, high above us. He talks to the students in *fusha* (classical Arabic) that only enhances the idolatry and praise unanimously shared in our ranks. For one hour, he teaches us a new tune, or we rehearse for the next *beet el 3ud* orchestra concert.

Once the *prova* is over, the sazs and the ouds are carefully packed away, while Um Mustafa, *beet el 3ud*'s guardian, takes away the last tea glasses left by the red velvet chairs. Some will choose to stay a little while longer to have a drink at Zainab el Khaitoun's... a little while that often turns into a whole night, which is why you can hear them singing until the wee hours.

# AFTER 8

TEXT: **MARWAN CHAHINE**

I learnt to love Egypt by getting to know those who didn't like it.
Or rather, those who preferred the nights of Cairo - its alcohol, its
women and men - to those of their home countries. This is the Cairo
of the Vampire-Egyptians, who gather nightly in one famous dark
room: After 8.

Back in 2011, one winter afternoon, Hassan whispered into my
ear: "Join me at After 8 around midnight." That day, we became
friends. It's hard to know anything personal about Hassan. It's also
hard to say how old he is. You can bump into him 24 hours a day,
wearing a neatly ironed shirt, alone or hand-in-hand with some good-
looking girl, near the Wust El Balad (downtown) cafes. He's easy
to spot thanks to his loyal companion, a gigantic vintage Cadillac,
which he takes special care to always park in everyone's way. Always.
That night, the Cadillac was taking pride in being parked in the
middle of the road, forcing other cars to detour around it. Their
drivers honked and yelled as they would have towards young girls.

At the entrance of a narrow alleyway, a sign with tired colours
pointed in the direction of After 8. My skepticism grew when I
recognised the powerful beats of 'Mister Vain' a tune I had listened
to compulsively back in the day. "En route for the 90s" I thought,

half-amused yet with a hint of condescension. Face-to-face with a bouncer smiling with malicious hypocrisy, my suspicion continued to rise. He seemed to say: Welcome, little bastard. We're gonna rip you off here. Today the waiters call me 'Mister,' but despite their coaxing and cajoling, I hold on to my first impression. And every time I come, they do rip me off.

I looked for Hassan across the poorly-lit room. The scenery was rather unexpected: brick walls, kitsch décor and a tiny dance floor. I had been afraid to stumble upon a snobbish crowd busy mimicking Western hipsters but instead found myself in the middle of a motley crew. Among them, a young guy in a semi-trance dancing to some sort of tectonic (I would later be told that these are electro shaabi grooves, a fusion of popular street tunes and hard core techno music, extremely popular in Egypt these past few years). A girl with a leopard headscarf stood on a table, beaming sensually to the music. Not far from her, a couple of obese dancers shook their hips with grace. Later I saw them in a full-mouth kiss - which is, as far as I know, unheard of in a public venue in Egypt. The cigarette smoke stung my eyes.

Without transition, the crackling speakers started to squeeze out salsa. I spotted Hassan spinning with a middle-aged white woman. Definitely a tourist. She seemed delighted to dance with him, despite her obvious difficulties to follow his lead and snake-like contortions. As soon as he caught sight of me, Hassan swiftly abandoned his dance partner and introduced me to his acquaintances - that is, more than two-thirds of those in the room. A TV anchor with an oddly straight lock of hair languishing on his forehead, surrounded by effeminate youth; a ballet dancer of sculptural beauty; a spirited chemist known for producing his own drugs; a left-wing activist freshly out of jail; an NGO worker who drinks down his shots of whisky as if it were water. All of the waiters take turns to ask my friend if he needs anything - is he okay, is he having fun, is he thirsty?

With their white shirts tucked into their trousers, their classical outfits contrast oddly with the baroque look of the place.

A French song was now playing. 'Johnny you're no angel' by Edith Piaf. I inquired about the DJ's surprising u-turns. Hassan replied crossly: "She's here every Tuesday. Believe me, she knows what she's doing." Dina is a tiny, fifty-something woman. She sports a boyish haircut and a loose black tee-shirt. She held a small green laser in her hand that she playfully pointed at dancers. They call her DJ Dina and seem delighted with her selection. But Dina is not only famous for her DJ skills: she has a history of complex political and personal choices. She was, for instance, one of the first Wust el Balad activists who openly voiced her criticism against Hosni Mubarak in the early 2000s.

The first notes of the next song were greeted with an impressive roar, though at first I didn't understand what the customers found so special about it. They jumped on the tables and windowsills, and shouted the lyrics in unison. I slowly realised that those were slogans, slogans that had been chanted just a hundred yards away on Tahrir Square. They demand the fall of the regime, bread, freedom, and social justice. The singer, whom at first I mistook for some uninspired bard, turned out to be the lead musician of the Egyptian revolution. He was on stage every day during the tumultuous and world-famous eighteen day uprising. Arrested and beaten up by police forces, Ramy Essam, a young guy from the Delta city of Mansura, quickly became a national symbol.

The song was over now but the shouts increased dramatically. The guardians of the night wouldn't give in: they would stay here until the wee hours, dancing, drinking, and hugging each other as if to make sure they're still alive.

# THIS IS CAIRO NOT THE SCREAMERS

TEXT: **ALAN BISHOP + HICHAM CHADLY**

Hicham Chadly was waiting to pick me up in his car at Al-Zahraa Metro Station. We were headed for the wastelands of West Cairo, on the outer side of the ring road where the streets are as bad as they get. We were looking for a wedding where a synth player from the delta - Hamada Moharram - that Chadly had contacted to discuss documenting him for Nashazphone's upcoming compilation 'This is Cairo, not the Screamers' - was performing with his band.

The area is a labyrinth of forgotten neighbourhoods left to die, a true third world Africa and it seems to never end in all directions. There was a thick layer of dust covering everything. Various old cars, tuk tuks imported from Thailand three years ago, buses, motorcycles and mini-buses kicked up that dust enough to create a fine misty fog in the chilled night air. Shops and small markets appeared along the way, nestled between mini downtown areas with bustling shops and cafes (even after midnight there were small business districts open with packed coffee houses, children playing on the streets and riding on broken down carnival swings and see-saws with the feel of a Saturday night at 8pm).

It was a continual scene from post-apocalyptic Hollywood. There were stretches where large apartment buildings flanked the road on both sides without a light in a window, each one looking unoccupied and unfinished - true desolation... a metropolis of ruin... of ruins... modern day ruins for a future archaeological dig. We had to ask directions almost every kilometre we travelled to confirm we hadn't made a wrong turn. The people were very kind, not one of them seemingly in judgment of whom we were and what we were doing there. Chadly did all the talking of course and everyone was cool - considering their treatment by Mubarak.

After almost an hour of trying to hunt down the location of this elusive wedding at the end of life on earth as many of us know it, we heard the music in the distance... that crazy synth serpentine tone coming from a well-lit area with coloured lights. "That must be it!" we thought. We accessed down a dirt road into another ruined zone of abandoned buildings mixed with half finished foundations and piles of bricks and parked. We strolled right into the rather small and modest gathering of hundred people and stood around watching for two minutes to get our bearings. The bride and groom with a swath of kids danced on the stage, while a synth player on the other side of the tent was bashing his keyboard, surrounded by his posse of friends, all of whom looked in their teens to early twenties.

Finally Hicham approached the sound man to ask the name of the group. It obviously wasn't our man on keyboards - we'd seen him in his YouTube videos - where Chadly first found his phone number, called and developed enough trust to get invited to this, the only wedding he would play near Cairo for the next seven months. He's from the Dekernes in the Delta and he plays almost exclusively there on a nightly basis. Sure enough, we were at the wrong wedding but Hicham got some basic, raw directions to the one we were looking for. The synth tones sounded great though and this guy was from the same basic scene. But he had no band and we were told there would be a full band present at the wedding we were hoping to find. We began driving further into the void and after a few more stops for directions and turning down various lanes that led to mysterious parts unknown, we heard the music once more, only this time as we approached the scene, the lights were brighter, the sound bigger, and the action greater.

As we pulled up to the spectacle there was a one hundred foot long gateway from the street into a huge covered venue decorated with multi-coloured flashing lights and a wildly coloured psychedelic entrance way. We parked across the street off the main road and walked straight past the assembled crowd at the gate, across beaten- down, filthy, dust-covered colourful rug after colourful rug, which pointed through atop the rocky dirt surface they covered directly into the main wedding area. All the while the music became louder and more intense as we came closer. It was a complete sensory overload assault- smoking pits of intoxicating meats, the sweet incense of massive stacks of fresh flowers, packs of men wearing expensive black suits, anarchistic waiters and henchmen moving around the venue serving anything and everything, table after table of lovely women seated to the left with the men along the right side, as we followed the filth carpet runway towards the front of the stage where we were greeted by a roving pack of young children running amok all over hell's half acre.

That's when we could finally stop, focus and stare at the spectacle blazing away in a fury right in front of us. There we were, witnessing the best, most interesting and happening music in all of Egypt and we were standing ten feet in front of centre stage with only a few random kids there with us. The volume was so loud that I couldn't tell if the speakers were distorted or if it was my ears that were damaged, which I know for a fact they are. The smell of flavoured shisha and grilled meats took hold, smothering the environment in ecstatic aromas. I pulled out my flash recorder and then noticed two open seats right at the front of the first table occupied by young men in their twenties and thirties. We asked if we could sit down and were kindly granted permission unanimously for the perfect location to be documenting such an event. The group consisted of seventeen members, although it was ambiguous with several men lurking on and around the stage at all times.

The instrumentation is as follows: Band leader/Synth #1 (our guy) – Drum Kit – electric bass guitar – two trumpets – trombone – seven frame drummers – two dunbeks – male vocalist – stage sergeant (MC who also sings and directs the wedding activities from the stage - he also screams a lot) – synth #2 – plus there were two female dancers who arrived later, along with the groom who took the stage and stayed for almost an hour. I pulled out the recorder, which looks enough like a cell phone to blend in, set it on the table and started recording audio. A while later when the dancers arrived, I pulled out the camera and shot about twenty-five minutes of the best segment they performed all night. Many kids and onlookers had assembled up front by then so it was easy to blend in and shoot video. I pulled out the swivel screen and held it up like an amateur, like someone who would buy an expensive camera and only use it for weddings and family engagements.

The wedding show was a full production. There were at least three cameras filming the event with one of them mounted on a mechanical crane that was operated by a man on the right side of the stage. The crane was about thirty feet long and angled up across most of the width of the stage as it moved up and down, swivelling to catch various image angle shots. There were two large video screens mounted from above on the left side of the stage, one was a high definition big-screen TV, and the other was an older big screen with a more washed out picture. The screens were projecting what the three cameras were shooting as the combination of images was being edited live for the wedding DVD by two men at a monitor/mixing station off the left side of the stage. One camera was exclusively making the rounds from table to table, shooting the guests accompanied by a light man. When they arrived at our table, I glanced at the big screen to see a huge close up of Chadly and I, my left eye almost entirely shut, expressionless face, looking like a villain from an old Bond flick. It was amazing. From now to eternity the wedding party will always wonder who the two guys were, sitting up front at that table... at their wedding! Other than the five men at our table, no one said a word to us or gave us a second look the entire time we were there. Various members of the wedding party continually walked by us, but there were neither looks nor even a glance.

The band leader synth player was the one who invited us but by the time we arrived, he was already performing and had no idea what we looked like as we had never met him, so we had no contextual reason to be there other than as wedding crashers... yet we ate and drank nothing. Stella beer was starting to get tossed on the tables and the kids up front were constantly being cleared away from the front of the stage by random men with sticks, shoeing away a swarm of house flies, the pests moving away and then back to the front with the waving of the hand... it was a fruitless endeavour to try to control them. There was a desk setup at right centre stage where two men sat and counted the hundred pound notes being tossed and flung into the air over the groom on stage (the money was then picked up and taken to the desk for processing). The cash was being donated to the groom and the name of the donor was repeated by the stage sergeant continually at the flinging of each bill over the groom's head one at a time.

There were true moments of ecstatic bedlam and frenzy, musically and vocally. And when the two dancers appeared in pseudo belly dance costumes, looking hot and slutty in that heavy-set skin showing kind of way, they began gyrating across the stage - the show rocketed towards the sky at this point as more random men took to the stage, cash was flying all over, trumpets blaring, the synth snaking and drums pounding with the vocalist and stage sergeant screaming at the top of their voices... well, you can now imagine. Around midnight, the band announced that they'd be performing for two more hours. Hicham had to split and work early in the morning. There was no chance to actually meet the synth player and so our faces and identities would remain anonymous. We left in a literal cloud of dust, as there had been some kids scuffling along the rug walkway and a hazy dirt odour filled the central part of the venue as we vanished underneath the chaos and drove away into the cool early morning breeze. We swerved and rocked along the horrific roads better suited for jeeps and camels through lively city drags that seemingly never ended. After one more stop for directions we finally received the correct advice and discovered the ring road once more.

# REROUTE

# MUIZZ STREET

TEXT: **TAMER FATHY**

PHOTOGRAPHY: **VIRGINIE NGUYEN HOANG**

Whenever I am walking through Muizz Street in the Hussein district on my way to the grand family house where I was born and grew up in, I am overwhelmed by a deep sense of longing for a time that has passed. Though I am only thirty-eight years old and moved, only seven years ago, to a place ten minutes away from El Hussein, in downtown Cairo, the feeling that I get from this district is something else altogether, like a warm embrace that envelops me again and again whenever I return. This is where my mother lived all her life and where my brother still lives. When I return, I feel the years falling away. I am a child again, sure of my place in the world.

The towering Fatimid mosques and ageless buildings tell me of my origins, my true self and my true age which is not thirty-eight years old, but thousands of years old - the owner of a wondrous legacy. When I was a child I did not realise that I played in the shadow of history. I find it incredible now that my playmates and I would so casually play hide-and-seek amongst significant historical monuments like the Sultan Kalawoon mosque, Wekalet Zaraa or the Seheimi house, without realising

what they were, before they were restored to the form they are in now.

Back then they were simply places to play. Back then I assumed all children could play in Fatimid bazaars and palaces. Now I realise how fortunate I was to grow up amongst these marvels of Islamic architecture.

My mother's family has always been from this area. My great grandfather was a Sufi Sheikh from Morocco who came to set up a school of Sufism and my mother's family was henceforth known as the 'Moroccans.'

My mother is a big part of why this district is so important to me - when I come to visit, now that she has passed away I see her everywhere. If I happen to hear Oum Kulthoum playing in a nearby café as I walk, my sense of her being present heightens even more. I recall how my mother accustomed me to listen to the special broadcast of Oum Kulthoum music at 5pm everyday. I also feel her presence when the call to prayer rings out during the day, the beautiful voices of the muezzins reverberating the ancient walls and melding with each other seamlessly.

A special place for me has always been the El Hussein Mosque

and especially the Om El Ghulam (Mother of the Boy) Mosque. My brother and I would go there often, especially when returning from my grandmother's house by Kasr El Shouq (the Palace of Desire), a district made famous by the Naguib Mahfouz novel. We would play there and then buy raw *Konafa* (vermicelli) and *Katayef* for my mother to prepare for us at home.

I've always loved the story behind this Mosque - this is where the woman who came from Kerbala with the head of El Hussein is buried, apparently she travelled all this way with the remains of the body and died on the spot, and the Mosque was erected in her honour. What is intriguing to me it that I have never found out if this story is true or not, but it is etched in my memory - indissoluble as only childhood stories are.

Later on in my adolescence I was obsessed with the Mosque of El Azhar. There was something about the courtyard's white facade and the alabaster pillars of the prayer hall that gave me a deep sense of ease - and it was always quite a sight to see masses of Azhar scholars passing to and from the Mosque all day - with their special *e'ma* hats, starched *galabeyas* and embroidered scarves flung over a shoulder.

I also loved it (though I discovered this much later) because it was a big part of the origins of Cairo. After all, Cairo was founded by Gawhar II Sicili, a Fatimid general of Sicilian extraction, and it was he who built the Mosque.

The city was called Il Mansuriya then - it was given the name El Qahera (Cairo) by the Caliph Muizz Li-Deen Illah, and the Mosque was known as the Mosque of Cairo. This was later changed to El Azhar by the second Fatimid Caliph Al Aziz Billah.

There are so many other places to see - El Muizz Street is rather vast, running from Bab El Futuh (Gate of Conquests) to Bab Zuweila, but it is also worth passing by the Aqmar Mosque and the Madrasa (school) of Sultan Ashraf El Barsbay.

These walls bear the history of my family's many generations and my name amongst them, to me this is not merely a place of exquisite architecture from the past, it is also an important and deep part of me.

# AN APPETITE FOR DOWNTOWN

TEXT: **GABI MANGA**

PHOTOGRAPHY: **MAGALI COROUGE**

Egypt is not a gastronomic wonder. To the north lies the Levant and sumptuous dishes of Falafel, Fattoush salads and proper uses of olive oil. To the west lies North Africa, filled with couscous, harissa, tagines and a medley of incredible dishes that reflect the region's Berber, Arab, Phoenician and French Colonial past. Egypt, situated between these two culinary powerhouses, has managed to produce local cuisine that is simply not up to snuff. I blame British colonialism for stunting its growth. Be that as it may, there are glimmers of hope.

The bourgeois of Cairo have abandoned downtown. While the neighbourhood could certainly use some restoration, it retains much of its charm from an era when it was the centre of Cairo's high society, and still permeates with its status as the centre of a truly cosmopolitan city. The architecture, cafes, antique shops, bars of Sherif, Adly, Tharwat and many of the other streets that lead in and out of Talaat Harb Square, are well worth a stroll on a Friday morning, sunset walk or night on the town. All of these activities will work up a hunger, and despite Egypt's lowly standing in the food realm, there are some delicious options.

## KAZAZ

After walking around on a hot day, or tying one on at Stella bar until the early morning hours, you will be in need of salty sustenance. Not everything on the menu is great, the foul (beans), for instance, are terrible. Kazaz, however, is home to one of the best lentil soups in the city. Add to this a gigantic and well-priced quarter chicken meal and you're in business. Other delicious favourites include the Basterma and Egg Sandwich (the closest you can get to bacon and eggs in Cairo) and the chicken Fattah (rice, fried pitta, tomato sauce, chicken shawarma). The dining area is air-conditioned, making Kazaz feel like a French-fry-tinged oasis come the summer months. In the Spring and Autumn take your meal to the nearby Borsa cafe district and enjoy the temperate Cairo weather and surprisingly gorgeous scenes of palm trees and downtown architecture. Don't buy any perfume or papyrus.

### SOMAYA'S

Located in an alley between Youssef El Gindy and Mohamed Sidy Streets (around the corner from Horreya Bar), Somaya's is not easy to find. Once you find it, you will be rewarded with one of the best dining experiences in Cairo. Somaya's, according to legend/my friend with a propensity for stretching the truth, was born out of the Revolution. The proprietor of the restaurant, Somaya herself, began to cook for the young revolutionaries of Tahrir Square during the January 25th uprising. So impressed with her cooking were they, that she was encouraged to start her own restaurant. While the Revolution has recently come into peril, Somaya's cooking remains amazing. Egyptian classics like Fasoulia, Mulukhia and Rice with Vermicelli, are done perfectly, alongside a rotating set of daily specials, including grilled chicken or meat cooked with tomato. Somaya's meats and vegetables are tender and miraculously well seasoned, beyond a rarity in Egyptian cuisine. Prices are extremely reasonable, and soda and tea can be ordered from the neighbouring cafe. While the restaurant is tiny, it is decorated with some of the most tasteful and simple furniture of any Cairo dining hall. Waitresses work on a volunteer basis and continue the youthful spirit of the restaurant's birth. Get there early as food usually runs out by 8:30pm. If you are lucky you may run into Somaya later in the night, dancing with friends at one of the surrounding venues of amusement.

## GRILLON

Located in an alley (are you getting that everything good downtown is hard to find?) off Mahmoud Bassiouny Street across from the Luxor Beer store, Grillon is another bar and restaurant that feels

like a relic from a bygone era. The clientele of lively aging middle-class secular men and women, often including former presidential candidate Khaled Ali, adds to the Nasser era vibe of the place, as does the grotto, waterfall, tropical plants and canopy roof. Waiters in waistcoats and bow ties are not the most responsive, but Grillon is a decent enough place to have a few drinks and relax without being bothered. There are only two things worth ordering at Grillon. One is the French Onion Soup. During the winter months Cairo becomes surprisingly cold and this soup, prepared au gratin, is a delicious guard against the brisk weather. You won't be making out with anyone that night, but your hunger will be quelled in a most tasty fashion. The only other thing worth ordering at Grillon is the Baladi Salad. This is essentially just tomato, cucumber, shredded lettuce and a bit of onion, however, it is consistently fresh and surprisingly good. Drizzle some lemon over the top and you will be delighted. That's it though. Don't order anything else at Grillon besides beer and shisha.

## OM DAHAB

Venture into the abyss once more, this time off Kasr el Nil Street, through the alley with the After 8 facade at its entrance. Yes, it looks sketchy. However, the light  at the end of the tunnel is a bustling cluster of cafes and shops, including the restaurant of one Miss Dahab. Essentially a food cart with three plastic tables alongside it,

Dahab is not going to bowl you over with amazement via her décor, but Dahab is feisty, warm and an amazing cook. There are a few core dishes that are always available, and always remarkable. Mulukhiyah, Fasoulia and spinach in spiced tomato sauce are your usual side options, perfect for mixing amongst Egyptian rice with vermicelli, and Mashi (peppers and leaves stuffed with rice) makes for a filling side dish. Dahab's signature dish is her chicken. Rubbed with salt and spices, and quickly fried in oil, its skin is the stuff of legend - crisp and flavourful, a decadent sin. As someone well versed in Cairo chicken, I can faithfully say that this is the city's best. A rather large meal for two will cost about forty Egyptian pounds. Drinks can be ordered from the waiter of the neighbouring cafe, and food is served promptly. There are no waiters at Dahab, so you are responsible for transporting dishes from the kitchen to your table.

Enjoy, my friends.

# ARD EL LIWA, UNNAMED AND UNPAVED

### OUR DAILY ROUTE FROM THE FOOTBRIDGE TO HOME, VIA THE CAFÉ AND MARKET.

TEXT: **MIRJAM LINSCHOOTEN**

PHOTOGRAPHY: **MIRJAM LINSCHOOTEN + SAMER FAROOQ**

Ard El Lewa is a busy labyrinth of unnamed and unpaved streets, where horse and donkey carriages, tuk tuks and motorbikes compete for space and attention. It is a world away from downtown. Yes, you will feel displaced, but it is welcoming and allows a look beneath the surface of Cairo.

When going to Ard El Lewa by taxi, do not tell the driver you want to go to Ard El Lewa. Taxi drivers will refuse to do so. Not because it is a dangerous place. Rather, one is to enter the neighbourhood by a pedestrian bridge, crossing an old railroad, from Sudan Street next to the KFC on the corner. Tell the driver instead you are going to 'Selim Elysées,' which is right at the footbridge and sounds a bit like 'Champs Elysées.'

When crossing the bridge you can feel the change from more reserved Mohandeseen into animated Ard El Lewa. Sometimes you can also feel the gushes of wind that make the bridge move.

When you arrive at the other side, descend the stairs to your right. You will face the front of the mosque and, if you

are lucky, tuk tuk drivers, sometimes no older than twelve years old, will be ready to take you around for no more than three Egyptian pounds.

But for now keep on walking. It is the best way to experience Ard El Lewa:

**1.** Take the first street to the left, on the right side of the mosque. On your left you will pass one of the smallest balconies in the world. On the right corner of the first crossing you can find good bananas. Continue straight until the end of the street, then take a right.

**2.** Take the first street left.

**3.** Take the first street right.

**4.** Take the second street left.

**5.** Turn right at the end. In the meantime, don't forget to look around.

**6.** Walk down the next street, a few metres before the end, to your left, you will find a reliable mirror shop where you can order any type of mirror, cut into any size on the spot. If you don't need a

mirror, just wave at the friendly owner drinking tea in front of his shop.

**7.** At the end of the street, before turning left, walk about fifty metres to the right to get a loaf of Fiteer bread and some lovely, fresh-baked cookies at the bakery. Walk back and take the first street on your right.

**8.** At about one hundred metres on the right, you will find the large Artellewa banner for the Artellewa Art Space. Artellewa hosts and organises exhibitions, workshops and other events in their gallery. Additionally, they have a weekly cinema programme, showing national and international films each Friday.

**9.** Next door to Artellewa is Donia's Hair Salon. A professional hair salon for women who wear a hijab, as well as for women without. If you don't need a haircut, owner Donia Mohamed can also offer you one of her beauty treatments, or simply a warm welcome in her women-only salon.

**10.** A little further down the street you will find 'the café.' There is no name for it, other than 'the café,' which is how everyone refers to it. Have tea (leave the complimentary glass of water), smoke a sheesha, play dominos or just sit and take in the neighbourhood.

**11.** For the market continue along and take the second street to your right. You will find the market on the second street to your left. You will know when you've found it. Here you can find household items, fruits and vegetables, as well as living animals for consumption such as fowl and rabbits. Continue along this street to the end, then turn left.

**12.** This is one of the main roads of Ard El Lewa with many shops and eateries. The second street on your left is the start of Mohamed Ali Al-Seary Street, which will take you back to where you came from, or you can hop on one of the many tuk tuks, with or without music installation.

ADDRESSES:

**MIRROR SHOP**

ATA AND EL-RAHEEM STREET, CLOSE TO AL
SHOHADA STREET
ARD EL LEWA, GIZA, EGYPT

**THE CAFÉ**

MOHAMED ALI AL-ESEARY STREET, A BIT
FURTHER DOWN FROM ARTELLEWA
ARD EL LEWA, GIZA, EGYPT

**BAKERY**

AL SHOHADA STREET, NEAR PALESTINE STREET
ARD EL LEWA, GIZA, EGYPT

**MARKET**

MAHER HAROUN STREET
ARD EL LEWA, GIZA, EGYPT

**ARTELLEWA ART SPACE**

19 MOHAMED ALI AL-ESEARY STREET
ARD EL LEWA, GIZA, EGYPT

**MAIN ROAD**

AL MOTAMIDIA STREET
ARD EL LEWA, GIZA, EGYPT

**DONIA'S HAIRSALON**

17 MOHAMED ALI AL-ESEARY STREET
ARD EL LEWA, GIZA, EGYPT

# FOOD DELIGHTS IN SATELLITE CITIES

TEXT: **NICHOLAS SIMCIK-ARESE**

PHOTOGRAPHY: **PASCAL MORA**

Any stroll through the crowded streets of Mohandiseen or Zamalek will reveal large billboards advertising a distant promised land. Green grass, pitched roof houses and flowing fountains frame joyous families running about or having picnics - the satellite cities of 6th of October! New Cairo! Through these opaque windows to enormous swaths of the city emerging from the desert there is "order" and "calm," or so we are promised.

While the fully integrated and privatised gated community is, in fact, a large part of reality in the desert fringes, and the 45-minute journey along the ring round feels daunting to the downtown-focused, they mask the unexpectedly rich and varied life and landscape of a more ephemeral crowd.

Beyond stereotypes of suburbanism, 6th of October is where students from all over the Egypt and the Arab world attend one of the eight universities, living away from home for the first time. It is where many Egyptians return to from long periods of migrant work abroad to invest new savings. In certain areas, it also where many of the city centre's urban poor have been resettled, into large public housing estates. Most distinctly, 6th of October has grown into the area of Cairo welcoming the largest numbers of refugees, those with some savings to put into a clean flat, while they wait for the tides of war or revolution to pass. The area is teeming with Iraqis, Libyans, Sudanese, and most recently many Syrians, looking to wait it out in an area that, perhaps a bit more than elsewhere, affords the possibility of starting a business.

This is why some of the best food from all over the region can be found here. It is without a doubt, the best place to catch a game of football, and it is a place where conversations across borders and class abound, all in such a public and communal setting that the billboards in Mohandiseen will feel more like a mirror reflection of the city inside, than a window to the outside.

**THE ROAD TO 6TH OF OCTOBER**

By taxi, ask any driver to take you to Hosary Square, 6th of October's implicitly recognised hub. At this point, you will have a choice of three routes: the 26th of July Corridor, the Southern Ring Road, or the Saft Al Laban Corridor. This last option provides a dramatic view from an overpass that slices through the entirety of Western Giza's hyper-dense quarters. Just past this you encounter the massive proliferation of dense, tall, perpetually growing construction at the rural edge. As you pop out of Saft of Laban, ask to get to October by heading South along the Ring Road. As the rural land breaks into desert, look left for a glance at the enormous pyramids poking up in the near distance. The journey shouldn't cost you more than sixty Egyptian pounds from Tahrir Square and is the most comfortable way out.

For a more varied and inexpensive (and much faster) experience, take a microbus from under 6th of October Bridge, by the Egyptian Museum. Just listen out for calls of October, October, October! or Hosary, Hosary, Hosary!, or ask any helpful microbus driver. The van will take you along the 26th of July Corridor, out of Giza and into the calm rural delta lands that buffer the city and finally through large swaths of desert and gated communities under construction. Along the desert stretches, look to your left for the National Police Mosque, a spaceship-like behemoth, emerging from the sands and a prime example of cyber-Islamic architecture. Later, past Sheikh Zaid City, look to your right for the Italian Circus, a series of mysterious, large, colourful tents along the roadside. As the landscape changes and the building becomes more dense, you will approach Hosary Mosque, which the driver should clearly announce upon arrival.

The journey is between three and five Egyptian pounds.

## HOSARY AREA

Hosary Mosque and Roundabout is the heart of 6th of October. This is the most convenient, and well-known, meeting place in town. It is also where the main microbus stand, to get to Giza or back downtown, is located, just opposite the mosque. East of the mosque, there is a large congregation of commercial buildings and street vendors. This is Tahrir Koshary, one of the best spots in the city for the delicious, traditional Egyptian high-carb staple of noodles, rice, lentils mixed in a spicy-vinegary tomato sauce and sprinkled with crispy onion flakes.

Behind this building, through one of several small alleys that lead through the row of shops, is Midan Amreeka (America Square). This space, brimming with outdoor cafes and shisha is the social heart of 6th of October. Head here between 7 and 10pm on a football match night, ideally during a major international tournament, to see cafes expanded to accommodate the swarms of Egyptian and refugee youth, hustling for seats amidst improvised projection screens, mounted throughout the square and hanging from building fronts. This outdoor makeover of public space allows one to watch several matches at once on huge screens, while shisha coal servers and waiters sprint through the square shouting out drink orders with an urgency, as if participants in the matches themselves.

Here you'll find people in their twenties from all corners of the Arab world, and an equally varied support for the teams, with loud chants and counter-chants abounding over several simultaneous matches. Add delicious juices, shisha and fresh coffees acrobatically brought to your seat in a heartbeat, and I can't think of a better way to watch football.

For a bite, the corners around Midan Amreeka contain some of the best Syrian restaurants in Egypt. All these businesses have popped up in the last two years, serving stellar abundant Syrian meals for the cost of a small shawarma sandwich in Zamalek. The wide selection of regional cuisine is well-worth exploring, but if there is time for only one try Hossam's Restaurant, in the eastern alley heading north from Midan Amreeka. This spot serves excellent Damascene cuisine onto a lovely front patio of tables, with flat bread wraps as their specialty. These restaurants act as an important hub for the Syrian community, employing many, and it is common to hear conversations comparing politics in Egypt and Syria.

## 7TH AND 1ST DISTRICTS

7th District (Hay al Sabbah) is just north of Midan Amreeka. About a ten- minute walk from the Syrian restaurants, on Mecca Al Mokarrama Street, is the Yordoon (Jordan) area. Here you will find an abundance of excellent Iraqi restaurants, owned and operated by exiles and refugees who have been moving to 6th October since the 2003 US led invasion of

Iraq. Try Iraqi specialities, such as a Kofte and tomato sandwich, or if feeling adventurous brain broth served in a goat's skull. Feel free to grab any food and eat it in any of the surrounding cafes that offer ample outdoor seating, provided you order a drink or a shisha. Tucked away further on the north western edge of 7th District, still on Mecca al Mokarrama St, is the Cairo office for the United Nations High Commission for Refugees (UNHCR). The building itself is heavily secured and cannot be visited without appointment, but its presence has an obvious impact on its local surroundings. In parks and squares around the site it is common to find Sudanese refugee communities camping out and selling goods, a combination of recent arrivals and asylum-seekers intermittently protesting in front of the office since 2006. Walking through this area you can sample some Sudanese coffee with ginger or try some Toombak, Sudanese dipping tobacco, and share a conversation about their journey and demands.

Further to the south, in the 1st District of 6th of October, look out for billiard halls frequented by many of the Palestinian, Syrian, Jordanian and Libyan medical and dentistry students, flat-sharing in the area. Order some excellent lemon juice with mint and ground ice. Have a shot at a pick-up game, or play dominoes and backgammon, and partake in conversations about great transition,

struggle and aspiration.

From a map and billboard, the satellite city of 6th of October may feel remote and sterile. Once here though, a bite and a chat will quickly remind you that in many ways, for many people, Umm Al Douniya, the mother of the world, is more than a referent to Cairo's past - it is also a promise.

# HOW TO GET FROM FAISAL TO TAHRIR

## *IN THE SLOWEST POSSIBLE WAY*

TEXT + PHOTOGRAPHY: **MAARTJE ALDERS**

One boiling mid-summer, freshly arrived in Cairo, I spent my first weeks in town with my friend Nesreen's family, in their crammed, cute apartment in Faisal. Faisal is at the far end of Giza, way out of reach of the two-line metro system, and the Egyptian equivalent of suburbia, a thunderous exploded version of provincial cities like Sohag or Assyut.

Parroting the people around me seemed to be the best survival strategy. So I happily sweated and swayed my way to downtown, next to my friend, on the popular microbuses.

Faisal Street runs from the pyramids to the Nile. My friend had this nifty trick of soaking her long sleeved shirt before setting off; something for which I was eternally grateful over the next 90 minutes, pressed against her arm in the front seat, on top of the engine in the sweltering weather.

To be honest, I think this activity will be most appealing for people to whom the word 'deathwish' has a certain charming ring. Besides being pushed, stared at and squeezed like a lemon, microbus drivers have an insatiable

need for speed. At the same time, I haven't found a more exhilarating way to move through the city. It's visceral, as if the city is trying to get into you, by shaking and honking and smelling as best as it can.

If you ever find yourself on the side of Faisal Street in need of a microbus trip, here is how to do it:

**GETTING IN**

Shout your destination at any bus passing by. Chances are the sound you produce is completely drowned out by the honks, beeps and braying donkeys. Do not worry, there is a highly developed system of hand gestures signifying different destinations that you can wave at drivers. To Tahrir, you wave your hand stretched out vertically up and down. If a bus is going there and there is space for you, it will pull over. There are different types of microbuses in each neighbourhood. Don't get caught up in trying to understand the difference. Just shout and gesture until someone pulls you in somewhere.

Once you find yourself on board, you are expected to pay one Egyptian pound. If you are on one of the four benches behind the driver, just tap the person in front of you on the shoulder and they will pass your coin forward. If you need change, it will come back to you in the same way. Avoid sitting directly behind the driver. You will not see a thing because you will be the one getting tapped on the shoulder and doing the accounts until you get off.

The driver might refuse to let you pay your one pound. In that case, don't think aaaaaah, they're so cute here, and leave it at that. I walked around with this false assumption of cuteness for about half a year, letting others pay for me, until I found out that it is customary to fight about bills. It's a national sport. It's politeness to say that don't have to pay, but in reality - pay. And don't worry about feeling pushy.

Actually, since this is not your every day routine, they will often make you sit up front, at least if you are a blonde, female foreigner. Maybe because they feel you need to be protected like a stray toddler, or that you are a nice extra edition to their flashy interior decoration. It's probably both. Enjoy sharing apples with the driver and having the city play itself out before you with the front window as a cinema screen.

A case could be made to experience the back seats though. There is a delicate dance of avoiding inappropriate touching between the opposite sexes.

Whenever a new person climbs on board, seating arrangements need to be reconsidered so that women passengers touch only each other. As a result, sometimes a new universe of being pressed between copious boobs and bums will unfold.

Now sit back, or recline into whatever position is available at the time, and enjoy. Sweat about how the hell you will alight, if you are neurotically inclined. Then consider this as therapy. My past small panics about getting out of trains back in Europe, have since disappeared.

## GETTING OUT

You can alight any time, anywhere. It's extremely efficient. Just shout at the driver and point at the side of the road. Making any kind of sound will work, and there is no need to master the Arabic phrase if your visit is very temporary.

Since we are heading to Tahrir, I will try to describe some main pointers to understand your progress. At the end of Faisal Street you will suddenly be catapulted onto a flyover that crosses the tracks of metro line 1, then you will plunge down past the back of Cairo University towards Behoos Square (you'll see the "horse statue"). This is the closest metro stop, so if you feel that at this point you desperately need a bathroom, plan your escape. If not, continue along Tahrir through Doqqi, towards the bridge over the Nile, to the southern tip of Zamalek island. After the Opera, you will cross another bridge, Qasr el Nil, that is flanked by lions, until you reach the Corniche. From here you will follow the Nile until the microbus main station under the flyovers of 6th of October bridge. Mission accomplished. Tahrir is the final destination, so just get off when you notice you are the last one left in the microbus. Walk away from the river with the Egyptian Museum (pink monstrosity) on your right, and head downtown for a well deserved Turkish coffee with cardamom.

Now to you, ladies, I have not been completely spared from the more unpleasant sides of living in Cairo as a woman, but in my experience people have been incredibly kind and helpful to me on those trips. When I started braving the bigger inter-neighbourhood buses, I had great fun discovering the feeling of a golden retriever hanging out of a car-window, experiencing an audience of loving smiles and inviting gestures whilst hanging from a handle bar, followed by a thunderous collective laughing fit and a cloud of waving hands when I wormed myself out at my destination.

Now, I live conveniently next to a metro stop and so, rarely take microbuses anymore. My confessions of their usage sparked a lot of hysterical laughter and popping eyeballs with other Egyptian friends, which I took as a nice excuse to adopt their local habit of taking the more convenient white taxis. But, there is no more delightful way to get introduced to this megalopolis. Just be sure to check the small print of your travel insurance.

# ARE YOU READY BOOTS?

TEXT: **KARIM RAHMAN**

PHOTOGRAHY: **PASCAL MORA**

Boots: no article of footwear is as diverse and as multipurpose as a good pair of boots. Be the chic, brown, strappy leather ones or a sturdy pair of Doc Martens, you can take boots out anytime, anywhere and on any occasion. In a city like Cairo, the big city that truly never sleeps (New York is a lie), where 'eclectic' is the plat du jour and the juxtaposition of scenery and culture is as commonplace as traffic, you need metamorphosing footwear to be able to adapt to the fast-paced change of scenery when going out on the town.

My train of thought when I wake up is - my boots, such a fabulous pair of brown, sturdy boots, deserve a fabulous day out, and no destination seems more appropriate than the glamorous, eclectic neighbourhood of Zamalek, and so it is there that I will head. A tiny island of lush greenery, classical architecture and gorgeous views of the Nile, Zamalek has an urban, metropolitan night scene as well; it is an Egyptianised Manhattan. With a Carrie Bradshaw-esque day planned out for me and my boots, no other area in Cairo fits the vivid image I have in mind. Rise and shine boots, it's time for a field trip!

First up - breakfast. You can't be fabulous on an empty stomach. The true beauty of Zamalek is best enjoyed by walking, not driving around the tiny suburbia. My boots and I find ourselves strolling down one of the area's more picturesque main streets, **ABO EL FEDA**, with its large canopy of green leaves filtering the sunlight down on us mere mortals, and the grand expanse of the Nile to our left.

I, of course, am heading nowhere but to the modern and urban it-place for a lovely breakfast meal - **LEFT BANK**. Situated (obviously) on the left bank of the historic river, the place is all glass and chrome and whitewashed walls, a vision of modern architecture and glamorous atmosphere. By the left wall, made entirely out of glass, offering the clientele a perfect view of the glittering waters and the symmetrical greenery, I sit down and order my go-to favourites: Vanilla Pancakes and a Cappuccino. They do not disappoint.

By lunchtime, my boots begin to get restless and so do I, so back to the streets we go. One of the many perks of Zamalek is the plethora of art galleries and concept stores randomly scattered around the island, so it's a great place to satisfy your inner cultural and artistic cravings. From **AMUSE** concept store to the **SAFAR-KHAN** art gallery on Brazil Street (my boots really enjoyed that one), the options are endless. By noon, you get to experience a different aspect of Zamalek. The seemingly quaint and peaceful district turns into a hub of activity and hustling inhabitants. Luckily, my boots adapt to the change quite nicely, transforming from a quaint and subtle accessory to a well-oiled machine, matching the fast-paced city life that blossomed around us. We found ourselves in front of **BLACKSTONE-BISTRO**, a contemporary American-styled bistro that boasts the best steak in Zamalek, situated on Taha Hussein Street, tucked away underneath the old-glamour **PRESIDENT HOTEL**. Clickety-clack go my boots as I walk into the restaurant, all dark wood and subdued mood; the perfect place to escape rush-hour Zamalek. An order of juicy rib-eye steak and a side of their freshly toasted garlic bread, **BLACKSTONE** managed to truly transport me to modern day Manhattan. My boots are appeased.

When night falls Zamalek undergoes its third and final transformation of the day, turning from a bustling metropolis to a flashy urban setting of bright lights and teeming nightlife. Where better to enjoy a fabulous drink than in **BAR'D'O?** Situated right next to Blackstone, tucked away like some ultra-exclusive club for fabulous people only, it's lucky I'm wearing my fabulous boots. Boasting simple and brutalist architecture, with bare,

dark-wood flooring, brick walls and frosted, stained-glass windows, **BAR D'O** immediately gives you a jazzy, New York circa 1920s vibe that makes you feel like Ella Fitzgerald at her most glamorous. Serving their colourful cocktails in 300ml jars and occasionally hosting some of Cairo's local Jazz talents, **BAR D'O** is the perfect way to end a fabulous day out in Cairo.

Boots: they work for breakfast, they work for a quick lunch or a business brunch and they work for a glamorous night out, and so does Zamalek. This tiny island of glamour has so much to offer, so put your boots on - Zamalek is definitely made for walking.

# STOLEN NOTES FROM
# LITTLE BLACK BOOKS

## SHOP

**KHAN EL KHALILI.** STOOLS, TABLECLOTHS, LAMPS, GLASSES, PLATES, CUSHIONS. BE PREPARED TO BARGAIN.

**UM EL DUNIA.** STOOLS, TABLECLOTHS, LAMPS, GLASSES, PLATES, CUSHIONS. NOT THE SAME PRICES AS IN THE KHAN BUT YOU WON'T HAVE TO BARGAIN.
*3 TALAAT HARB ST. DOWNTOWN. TEL: 0223938273.*

**SOUK EL FUSTAT.** BEAUTIFUL HANDMADE FURNITURE, ACCESSORIES, CLOTHES AND MORE.
*MAR GIRGIS ST. OLD CAIRO.*

**SAMIR'S ANTIQUE SHOP** FOR FILM POSTERS, GIGANTIC GRAMOPHONES & VINTAGE DISKS.
*METRO TOWERS, 2ND FLOOR, ZAMALEK.*

**ZAFIR.** FUNKY T-SHIRTS BY TALENTED EGYPTIAN DESIGNERS. ASK TO BE TAKEN INSIDE TO THE TREASURE TROVE OF KNICK-KNACKS, ACCESSORIES AND JEWELRY, CELEBRATING ALL THINGS CONTEMPORARY AND EGYPTIAN.
*15, TAHA HUSSEIN ST. ZAMALEK.*

**BEADS AND THREADS.** HAND EMBROIDERED SCARVES, KAFTANS AND JEWELRY. YOU CAN HAVE A BESPOKE DRESS MADE IN A WEEK (FOR VERY CHEAP) AT THE ATELIER INSIDE.
*10 EL MESSAHA SQ. DOKKI. TEL: 0237483287.*

**AZBAKIA MARKET** (ATABA) HUGE SECOND HAND BOOK MARKET. LOOK OUT FOR OLD MOVIE POSTERS, PAINTINGS STAMPS AND COINS.

## EAT AND DRINK

**FALAK CAFE** IS THE LATEST ADDITION TO A RATHER QUIET NEIGHBOURHOOD. SET IN A TASTEFULLY DECORATED FLAT, WITH A TYPICAL GARDEN CITY FLAVOUR, YOU CAN BE SERVED COPIOUS BREAKFASTS AND TASTY LATTES, SALADS, CREPES AND HAMBURGERS. YOU WILL ALSO FIND PAINTINGS MADE BY SHAYMA KAMEL, THE OWNER OF THE PLACE, POTTERY FROM FAYOUM, BOOKS AND ALL SORTS OF SOUVENIRS.
*ADDRESS 7 GAMAL EL DIN ST., GARDEN CITY.*
*OPEN DAILY 10AM-11PM.*

**KAKAO**. THE BEST ESPRESSO IN TOWN IS TO BE FOUND BEHIND THE ITALIAN EMBASSY IN GARDEN CITY. THEY ALSO SPECIALIZE IN POLITICAL CHOCOLATES. *2 EL ZAEEM EL HENDY GHANDY ST, GARDEN CITY. TEL: 01003000180.*

**GREEK CLUB** IS WELL KNOWN FOR ITS GREEK SALADS, ITS OUZO AND ITS DECADENT WEEKEND NIGHTS WITH A GREEK WEDDING FLAVOUR.
*OFF TALAAT HARB SQ. TEL: 0225750822.*

**ESTORIL** IS A SMOKY INFORMAL HQ FOR THE LIBERALS DOWNTOWN, SERVES DECENT BABAGHANOUJ AND SPINACH CANNELLONI.
*12 TALAAT HARB ST. TEL: 0225743102.*

**STELLA BAR** IS A LATE NIGHT INSTITUTION DOWNTOWN. BEERS ONLY. BEWARE, THE WOMEN'S BATHROOM IS THE SMALLEST IN EGYPT.
*BEHIND THE KIOSK AT THE CORNER, OFF TALAAT HARB ST. AND HUDA SHARAWI ST. TEL: 0223921067.*

**ITALIAN CONSULATE** (NASSER) FOR THE ANTIPASTI AND THE CHIANTI. BEST DURING SUMMER MONTHS WHEN THE TABLES ARE OUTSIDE. 15LE CHARGE FOR NON-ITALIAN COSTUMERS. *24 EL-GALAA ST. ENTER THROUGH THE GARAGE DOOR. TEL: 0227730109.*

**LEFT BANK**. FOR AN EXPENSIVE BRUNCH WITH A PRICELESS NILE VISTA. BEST TO GO EARLY ON WEEK-ENDS: THEIR BRUNCH FORMULA IS VERY POPULAR. THE STAFF ISN'T AS GREAT AS YOU WOULD IMAGINE, BUT THE EGGS BENEDICT ARE.
*53 ABU EL FEDA ST. TEL: 0227350014.*

**FRENCH INSTITUTE** (MOUNIRA) FOR THEIR RELAXING INDOOR GARDEN AND A POULET MOUTARDE. LUNCH ONLY. *IN A TINY STREET OFF KASR EL AINI ST. TEL: 0227350014.*

**ABU TAREK** FOR A TRULY SOPHISTICATED KOSHARY EXPERIENCE, ALSO KNOWN AS 'THE KOSHARY KING'. TOMATO SAUCE AND GRILLED ONIONS SERVED ON THE SIDE IN SILVER DISHES. IT DOESN'T GET ANY BETTER THAN THIS.
*CHAMPOLLION ST. DOWNTOWN. TEL: 0225775935.*

**WINDSOR HOTEL** (ATABA) PERFECT FOR A 10PM COCKTAIL AND A SNACK. REMINISCE OVER THE BRITISH ERA IN THEIR SPLENDID VINTAGE LIVING ROOM.
*ALFI BEY ST. OFF 26TH JULY (ATABA). TEL: 0225915810.*

**EL GAHSH**. BEST TO VENTURE OUT WITH AN EGYPTIAN VOLUNTEER, BUT FOR THE MORE DOWN-AT-HEEL EXPERIENCE PAR EXCELLENCE, THIS IS NOT TO BE MISSED. POSSIBLY THE BEST FAVA BEAN STEW ON THE PLANET. DON'T INQUIRE TOO CLOSELY ABOUT WHAT'S IN IT.
*STALL LOCATED PARALLEL TO SAYEDA ZEINAB MOSQUE.*

**EL BORG**. THE DECOR MAY BE IN AMUSINGLY BAD TASTE BUT THE FISH CERTAINLY ISN'T. HAILING ORIGINALLY FROM THE MARITIME CITY OF PORT SAID, EL BORG IS ONE OF THE FEW REASONS TO TREK OUT TO NASR CITY AND IS WELL WORTH IT.
*2 ABDULLAH EL ARABY ST. NASR CITY. TEL: 01005466626.*

ZOOBA IS A VERY ENTERTAINING CANTINE WITH CREATIVELY TWISTED EGYPTIAN DISHES. PINK AND GREEN BREAD LOAVES A MUST!
*26TH JULY ST. ZAMALEK. TEL: 01023152510.*

# LIVE MUSIC AND DANCING

MAKAN. 'THE PLACE' IS A TINY, CHARMING ONE-ROOM CONCERT HALL, WITH A BALUSTRADE AND POSSIBLY ONE HUNDRED PLACES MAXIMUM, LOCATED ACROSS FROM THE SAAD ZAGHLUL MAUSOLEUM. COME EARLY ON TUESDAYS (7PM) FOR THE PLACE IS FAMOUS FOR ITS TRADITIONAL UPPER-EGYPT MUSIC ENSEMBLE, MAZAHER. YOU MIGHT GET INTO A TRANCE ALONG WITH THE GOD-LIKE NUBIAN SINGERS! TEA AND KARKADE ARE OFFERED AT THE INTERMISSION. 30LE COVER.
*1 SAAD ZAGHLUL ST. MOUNIRA.*

ARAB MUSIC INSTITUTE IS WORTH VISITING IF ONLY FOR THE PLACE ITSELF. IN THIS RECENTLY RESTORED 1920S PALACE IS NESTLED THE MOST BEAUTIFUL, LITTLE KNOWN, CONCERT HALL IN CAIRO. CHECK THE OPERA WEBSITE FOR MORE INFORMATION AS THE SCHEDULE IS IRREGULAR: WWW.CAIROOPERA.ORG
*RAMSES ST. DOWNTOWN.*

AFTER 8 TUESDAYS ARE A MUST HERE THANKS TO DJ DINA'S ECLECTIC MIX OF EGYPTIAN, ENGLISH AND FRENCH CLASSICS. DON'T COME BEFORE 11PM. COVER: 60LE. *KASR EL NIL ST. DOWNTOWN.*

VENT IS BOTH AN EDGY SCREENING PLACE AND A POPULAR DANCE-FLOOR WHERE THEME NIGHTS USUALLY END AROUND 4AM.
*KASR EL NIL ST. DOWNTOWN.*

AFRICANA. TIRED OF DOWNTOWN? HOP IN A CAB ALL THE WAY TO THE PYRAMIDS AND ENTER THIS HIDDEN WORLD KNOWN TO HAVE THE BEST MUSIC IN TOWN. BEST FOR GIRLS TO BE ACCOMPANIED BY MALE FRIENDS.
*HARAM STREET, GREATER GIZA.*

# TRY

*1 BASBOUSA* AT SIMONDS, ORIENTAL SWEETS AT LA POIRE OR EL ABD (DOWNTOWN), FRESHLY GROUND COFFEE AT CAFE BRAZIL (DOWNTOWN), *1 FOUL* PLATE FOR BREAKFAST, *FETEER* (THE SUGARY KIND), *MULUKHIYYEH*, STELLA BEER, STUFFED PIGEON, SHEESHA.

# TAKE BACK

A TAILORED SUIT (FROM ATABA), A BOTTLE OF JASMINE SCENT (TALAAT HARB SQ.), A *TAOWLA* GAME, AN UM KALTHUM DISK, A NADIA LOTFI POSTER, A 2-GUINEA EGYPTIAN FLAG (TAHRIR SQ.), A PHOTO OF THE MOHAMED MAHMOUD GRAFFITI.

# LET OFF STEAM

**EL AZHAR PARK** (OLD CAIRO) NO DOUBT YOU WILL BE CRAVING FOR GREEN SPACE AT SOME POINT. A LONG WALK IN EL AZHAR PARK IS A SIMPLE AND EFFICIENT WAY TO RELAX IN CAIRO, ESPECIALLY IF YOU SIT DOWN AT THE CAFE OVERLOOKING THE POND. ENTRANCE FEE FOR NON-EGYPTIANS: 10LE. A TRIP TO THE **CITADEL** WILL REMIND YOU HOW HORIZONTAL CAIRO IS. YOU CAN VISIT A FOURTEENTH CENTURY MOSQUE, MUHAMMAD ALI'S TOMB AND ADMIRE THE CITY INSIDE THE CITY BUILT BY SALADIN, OR SIP A COFFEE IN FRONT OF THE BEST PANORAMA IN TOWN. COVER FEE: 50LE. *OPENING HOURS: SUNRISE TO SUNSET.*

ACROSS FROM THE **FOUR SEASONS HOTEL**, ON THE CORNICHE (GARDEN CITY), YOU WILL SPOT THE LONG THIN **FELUCCA** SAILS. GO DOWN A FEW STEPS, ASK FOR A ONE HOUR RIDE (FIXED PRICE: 60LE FOR ONE BOAT). THERE IS ROOM FOR UP TO 15 PEOPLE PER FELUCCA. IT'S BEST TO GO AT SUNSET. YOU CAN BRING YOUR OWN DRINKS AND SNACKS.

ALTHOUGH IT IS NOT A TYPICAL EGYPTIAN HOBBY, THERE ARE STILL FINE HAMAM OPTIONS TO BE DISCOVERED IN CAIRO. **DAR EL MAGHREB** IS A GOOD COMPROMISE BETWEEN A COMFORTABLE AND A GENUINE MOROCCAN EXPERIENCE. BRING YOUR SHAMPOO AND OTHER BATH PRODUCTS, AND A SWIMSUIT IF YOU NEED ONE. ROBE AND SLIPPERS PROVIDED. 150LE FOR A BASIC SCRUB AND WASH FORMULA.*16, SALAH EL DIN MOSTAFA ST. MOHANDISEEN. TEL: 0233355925.*

**INDONESIAN EMBASSY.** TIRED OF THE EGYPTIAN STREET-FOOD TRIO (FOUL, KOSHARY AND FALAFEL)? THEN YOUR MOST ACCESSIBLE GATEWAY IS DEFINITELY THE WEDNESDAY LUNCHES AT THE INDONESIAN EMBASSY. FOR LESS THAN 30LE, YOU WILL GET SOUP, FRIED FISH OR CHICKEN SATAY, RICE AND DESSERT. COME EARLY - THIS IS A POPULAR OPTION AMONG FOREIGNERS WORKING IN THE NEIGHBOURHOOD. *13, AISHA EL TAIMOURIA ST. GARDEN CITY.*

A GOOD OPTION FOR FRIDAY LUNCHES IS **GENGIS KHAN**, IN *MAADI (ROAD 208, DEGLA)*. TUCKED INSIDE A CHARMING, YELLOW HOUSE, WHERE STRAY CATS PLAY IN THE YARD, THIS RESTAURANT SERVES THE MOST SUBTLE ASIAN FOOD IN CAIRO. RUN BY THREE GENERATIONS OF CHINESE WOMEN, IT OFFERS GENEROUS PORTIONS. A PLUS - RIOJA AND PINOT NOIR ARE ON THE WINE LIST. ON YOUR WAY BACK, ENJOY THE AREA'S QUIET STREETS, ADMIRE SOME OF THE LA-STYLE HOUSES AND BROWSE IN ONE OF THE SEVERAL WELL-STOCKED MAADI BOOKSHOPS: **KOTOBKHAN** *(EL LASILKY ROAD)*, **THE BOOKSPOT** *(ROAD 9)* OR **DIWAN** *(ROAD 254)*.

# MUSEUMS AND ART GALLERIES

**THE NATIONAL MUSEUM** IS THE KING OF ALL MUSEUMS IN CAIRO. YOU CAN'T MISS THIS MASSIVE PINK-STONED BUILDING ON THE VERGE OF TAHRIR SQUARE. GET LOST IN ITS LONG DUSTY ALLEYWAYS. IF YOU'RE BRAVE ENOUGH, YOU'LL PAY A LITTLE EXTRA TO VISIT THE MUMMIES SPECIAL ROOM. BEST TO VISIT IN THE MORNING IF YOU CAN: CLOSING HOURS HAVE BEEN RATHER CHAOTIC SINCE 2011. 60LE ENTRANCE FEE FOR NON-EGYPTIANS. *TAHRIR SQUARE, DOWNTOWN.*

CONTEMPORARY ART IN THE DESERT? AN UNLIKELY CONCEPT MADE POSSIBLE BY THE **ADAM HENEIN MUSEUM**, ON THE ROAD TO THE GIZA PYRAMIDS. ADAM HENEIN IS ONE OF EGYPT'S MOST FAMOUS LIVING PAINTERS AND SCULPTORS. YOU WILL ENJOY THE SPACIOUS WHITE ROOMS AND THE RELAXING GARDENS AS MUCH AS HENEIN'S BRONZE STATUETTES.
*OPENING HOURS: 11AM - 4PM. CLOSED ON WEDNESDAYS AND THURSDAYS.*
*CHECK OUT THE USEFUL DIRECTIONS ON THEIR WEBSITE: WWW.ADAMHENEINMUSEUM.COM.*

**TOWNHOUSE GALLERY** IS A BUSTLING EXHIBITION CENTRE AND SCREENING SPACE. EVERY MONTH, IT HOSTS THE LAUNCH OF TOK TOK, A POPULAR COMIC BOOK MAGAZINE. YOU CAN FIND SECOND HAND BOOKS, MAGAZINES AND POSTCARDS IN THEIR TINY BOOKSHOP AND PAUSE FOR A COFFEE OR A *KARKADE* IN ONE OF THE NEARBY OUTDOOR CAFES.
*OFF CHAMPOLLION STREET, DOWNTOWN.*

**BEIRUT** IS A RECENTLY OPENED EXHIBITION SPACE LOCATED IN A LATE 1940S THREE-STOREY HOUSE, IN THE QUIET NEIGHBOURHOOD OF AGOUZA. THE TEAM CURATES SHOWS WITH BOTH LOCAL AND INTERNATIONAL ARTISTS, AND WORKS ON SEASONAL THEMES THROUGH RESEARCH PROJECTS. IT'S WORTH STROLLING AROUND BY THE NILE TO TAKE A LOOK AT THE HOUSEBOATS, POPULAR IN THIS AREA.
*OPENING HOURS: SUNDAY TO THURSDAY, 10AM - 8PM.*
*11 ROAD 12 MAHMOUD SEDKY, AGOUZA. WWW.BEIRUTBEIRUT.ORG*

**AGRICULTURE MUSEUM** SOUNDS BORING TO YOU? IT SHOULDN'T. LOCATED IN A PRINCESS PALACE, THIS 1930 MUSEUM DISPLAYS ODD COLLECTIONS SUCH AS WAX MODELS OF TYPICAL EGYPTIAN MEALS, TAXIDERMY ANIMALS (INCLUDING A LION), DIGESTION DISPLAYS - CHECK THAT COW'S STOMACH! - AND ANATOMICAL MODELS.
*WEZARET EL ZARAA ST. DOKKI.*

# BEACHES, OASES AND ESCAPADES

**SAQQARA PYRAMIDS** OLDER AND PRETTIER THAN THE WORLD FAMOUS GIZA PYRAMIDS.

**EIN SUKHNA** IS BY FAR THE CLOSEST SEA SPOT YOU CAN FIND FROM CAIRO - ROUGHLY A TWO HOUR CAR RIDE DEPENDING ON TRAFFIC. AN ARRAY OF ALL-INCLUSIVE HOTELS HAVE COLONISED THE SHORE; THEY OFFER ACCESS TO A HANDFUL OF PRETTY BEACHES WHERE YOU CAN SWIM, SNORKEL OR SAIL. CAIRENES USUALLY GO FOR A NIGHT OR FOR THE DAY, EVEN THOUGH HIGH-SEASON WEEK-ENDS CAN BE CROWDED.
*STELLA DI MARE HOTEL, HURGHADA EL AIN EL SOKHNA RD. TEL: 0623250300.*

YOU CAN REACH THE **FAYOUM OASIS** IN THREE HOURS IF YOU'RE LUCKY TRAFFIC-WISE. PERFECT FOR A TWO-DAY TRIP, YOU CAN EITHER STAY IN ONE THE TWO ECO-LODGES IN THE TOWN OF TUNIS BY THE LAKE QARUN, OR GO SLEEP IN THE NEARBY DESERT WITH BEDOUINS WHO WILL DRIVE YOU AROUND, COOK AND SET UP A TENT FOR YOU. THE FAYOUM POTTERY IS AS FAMOUS AS ITS DESERT, DON'T OVERLOOK IT!
*ZAD EL MUSAFER ECOLODGE, QAROUN LAKE ROAD EZBET TUNIS. TEL: 0846820180.*

# CONTRIBUTORS

**MAARTJE ALDERS** IS A PRODUCER IN CAIRO BY DAY AND PHOTOGRAPHER BY NIGHT. THOUGH SLIGHTLY RESERVED AT FIRST, SHE IS GENERALLY ENTHUSIASTIC. SHE'S BEEN SPOTTED ALL OVER EUROPE WITH RECENT SIGHTINGS IN EGYPT.

**AHMED AMIN** IS A WRITER AND FILMMAKER WHO BELIEVES THAT WALKING WITH MUSIC IN YOUR HEADPHONES WILL TEACH YOU MORE THAN ALL THE WORLD'S LIBRARIES COMBINED.

**FRANÇOISE BEAUGUION** GRADUATED FROM THE NATIONAL SCHOOL OF PHOTOGRAPHY IN ARLES IN 2009. SHE CURRENTLY LIVES AND WORKS IN CAIRO.

**ROBERT BESHARA** (MFA GOVERNORS STATE UNIVERSITY) IS AN ACADEMIC AND AN ARTIST. AS AN ACADEMIC HIS AREAS OF RESEARCH INCLUDE FILM STUDIES AND TRANSPERSONAL PSYCHOLOGY. AS A FILMMAKER HIS WORK HAS BEEN SHOWN AT THE NEW YORK INTERNATIONAL FILM & VIDEO FESTIVAL, EL SAWY INTERNATIONAL FILM FESTIVAL, THE INTERNATIONAL ARTEXPO, THE ONE-MINUTE FILM FESTIVAL, THE CHICAGO INTERNATIONAL MOVIES AND MUSIC FESTIVAL, AND THE DUBAI INTERNATIONAL FILM FESTIVAL.

**ALAN BISHOP** IS AN AMERICAN MUSICIAN, MOST FAMOUS FOR BEING THE BASSIST AND VOCALIST OF EXPERIMENTAL ROCK BAND SUN CITY GIRLS. HE IS ALSO THE CO-FOUNDER OF THE LABEL SUBLIME FREQUENCIES, A SEATTLE-BASED RECORD LABEL FOCUSED ON RELEASING ESOTERIC MUSIC AND IMAGERY FROM ALL OVER THE WORLD, MOST NOTABLY FROM SOUTHEAST ASIA, NORTH AFRICA AND THE MIDDLE EAST.

**HICHAM CHADLY** IS ALGERIAN-EGYPTIAN AND LIVES IN CAIRO. HE IS THE FOUNDER OF THE EXPERIMENTAL RECORD LABEL NASHAZPHONE AND A FREQUENT COLLABORATOR OF SUBLIME FREQUENCIES FOR WHICH HE HAS COMPILED 1970S ALGERIAN PROTO-RAI UNDERGROUND AND 1970S ALGERIAN FOLK AND POP.

**MARWAN CHAHINE** IS A FRENCH JOURNALIST LIVING IN CAIRO WHERE HE WIDENS HIS KNOWLEDGE OF THE CAPITAL'S NIGHTLIFE BY HANGING OUT IN DINGY BARS, ALLEGEDLY TO UNDERSTAND THE SECRET OF THE PYRAMIDS.

**AUGUSTO COMÉ** SPENT YEARS WANDERING THROUGH THE FORMER SOVIET UNION. HE THEN MOVED TO CAIRO. WHEN NOT MONITORING ELECTIONS, HE TRAINS TO BECOME A PROFESSIONAL BACKGAMMON PLAYER.

**MAGALI COROUGE** IS A FREELANCE PHOTOJOURNALIST BASED IN CAIRO SINCE 2012. SHE IS A FREQUENT CONTRIBUTOR TO LE MONDE, LE PELERIN, JEUNE AFRIQUE, COURRIER INTERNATIONAL, DER SPIEGEL, THE FINANCIAL TIMES AND INTERNATIONAL ORGANISATIONS SUCH AS UNESCO.

**WAEL ESKANDAR** IS AN INDEPENDENT JOURNALIST AND BLOGGER BASED IN CAIRO. HE IS A FREQUENT COMMENTATOR ON EGYPTIAN POLITICS AND HAS WRITTEN FOR AHRAM ONLINE, EGYPT INDEPENDENT, DAILY NEWS EGYPT, COUNTERPUNCH AND JADALIYYA. HE HAS ALSO CONTRIBUTED TO THE KAZEBOON MOVEMENT. ESKANDAR HAS MADE MEDIA APPEARANCES FOR AL JAZEERA, RUSSIA TODAY, AND ALHURRA. HE BLOGS AT NOTESFROMTHEUNDERGROUND.NET.

**NURAH FARAHAT** IS AN AWARD WINNING FILMMAKER AND PHOTOGRAPHER. SHE LIKES OCTOPUS, NUMBERS AND TAKING CARE OF HER PLANTS.

**TAMER FATHY** IS A CHOREOGRAPHER, DANCER AND SCREENWRITER BUT WOULD MUCH RATHER BE ON A FARM WITH A DOZEN CHILDREN. TILL THEN HE'LL MAKE DO WITH THE FRIENDLY GHOST SHARING HIS DOWNTOWN FLAT.

**DALILA GHODBANE** IS AN ARCHITECT AND URBAN PLANNER WHO HAS LIVED IN PARIS, BEIRUT AND CAIRO. SHE TELLS FICTIONS BASED ON TRUE URBAN FACTS.

**MONICA HANNA** IS AN EGYPTOLOGIST WHO BELIEVES THAT ANTIQUITIES ARE NOT JUST FOR TOURISTS AND THE ELITE, BUT FOR ALL EGYPTIANS. SHE HAS STUDIED AT THE AMERICAN UNIVERSITY IN CAIRO, THE UNIVERSITY OF PISA AND IS CURRENTLY A JUNIOR POST DOCTORAL FELLOW AT HUMBOLDT UNIVERSITY OF BERLIN.

**AHMED HEGAB** IS A DIGITAL MEDIA TRAINER, BLOGGER, PHOTOGRAPHER, WINNER OF TWO NATIONAL GEOGRAPHIC PHOTO CONTESTS AND CO-FOUNDER OF MESHABBEK - A PLATFORM FOR EGYPTIAN ARTISTS.

**MARWAN IMAM** WAS CLASSICALLY TRAINED IN THE ART OF MECHANICAL ENGINEERING AND THE SCIENCE OF FINE ARTS. HE IS A FILMMAKER, COMIC BOOK ARTIST, PHOTOGRAPHER AND MUSICIAN. NOBODY KNOWS HOW HE MANAGES TO PRODUCE EVERYTHING HE DOES BUT IT IS RUMOURED HE HAS A SWEATSHOP IN TAIWAN.

**LAYLA ISKANDAR** IS SEVENTY YEARS OLD. SHE DOESN'T FEEL SO IN HER MIND, BUT DOES SO IN HER KNEES. SHE IS A FRENCH AND SOCIOLOGY TEACHER IN CAIRO AND LIVES IN HELIOPOLIS, THE CITY OF THE SUN, THAT SHE LOVES TO TALK ABOUT.

**SVEN KARNGÅRD** IS A WRITER WHO SUFFERS FROM A RARE CONDITION, GRADUALLY TURNING HIM INTO FICTION. CAIRO ISN'T EXACTLY SLOWING THE PROCESS DOWN.

**MIRJAM LINSCHOOTEN** (FRANCE) AND **SAMEER FAROOQ** (CANADA) BEGAN THEIR ARTISTIC COLLABORATION WHILE STUDYING AT THE GERRIT RIETVELD ACADEMIE IN AMSTERDAM. THEIR WORK OFTEN (BUT NOT ALWAYS) ADDRESSES THE CONSTRUCTION OF KNOWLEDGE THROUGH PROPOSING ALTERNATIVE SYSTEMS OF LOOKING, ORDERING AND DISPLAY. THE ARTISTS HAVE EXHIBITED INTERNATIONALLY IN TURKEY, CANADA, USA, FRANCE, THE NETHERLANDS, BELGIUM, SWITZERLAND, CHINA AND EGYPT.

**GABRIEL LUIS MANGA** IS A SOCIAL ENTREPRENEURSHIP CONSULTANT AND A CONNOISSEUR OF THE SMALL DETAILS OF LIVING IN CAIRO. HE IS AWARE THAT NOT ALL CULINARY MAINSTAYS, MICROBUS MODELS AND TAILORS ARE CREATED EQUAL, AND HAS AN EYE FOR THE SUBTLE BUT IMPORTANT DISTINCTIONS BETWEEN THEM. CAIRENES ARE OFTEN AMUSED BY HIS LAST NAME, WHICH MEANS MANGO.

**PASCAL MORA** WAS BORN IN 1983 IN SWITZERLAND. HE IS A FREELANCE PHOTOGRAPHER, SPECIALISED IN PORTRAITURE AND REPORTAGE. HE LIVES AND WORKS IN CAIRO AND ZÜRICH.

**EBADA NAGUIB** IS A FILM DIRECTOR AND A VISUAL ARTIST. SHE THINKS SHE REALLY SHOULD HAVE BEEN A CONSUMPTIVE 19TH CENTURY ENGLISH POET BUT IS CONTENT OTHERWISE.

**VIRGINIE NGUYEN HOANG** IS A BELGIAN PHOTOJOURNALIST BASED IN CAIRO. SHE CURRENTLY WORKS FOR THE EGYPTIAN ONLINE NEWSPAPER MADA MASR. A CONTRIBUTOR AT STUDIO HANS LUCAS, SHE IS ALSO A STRINGER FOR AGENCE FRANCE PRESSE (AFP). SHE HAS CREATED THE HUMA COLLECTIVE WITH PHOTOGRAPHERS FRÉDÉRIC PAUWELS AND GAËTAN NERINCX, WHICH AIMS AT FOCUSING ON SOCIAL ISSUES AND A HUMANIST APPROACH OF PHOTOGRAPHY.

**XENIA NIKOLSKAYA** IS A VISUAL ARTIST, WORKING MAINLY IN PHOTOGRAPHY. BORN IN LENINGRAD (SAINT-PETERSBURG, RUSSIA), SHE LIVES BETWEEN MOSCOW, CAIRO AND STOCKHOLM. SHE IS A CONTRIBUTOR FOR SEVERAL MAGAZINES INCLUDING: NEWSWEEK, GEO AND CONDÉ NAST TRAVELLER. SHE IS WIDELY EXHIBITED IN DIFFERENT MUSEUMS AND ART INSTITUTIONS SUCH AS THE ARAB INSTITUTE IN PARIS, THE MEDITERRANEAN CULTURE MUSEUM OF STOCKHOLM AND MATHAF: ARAB MUSEUM OF MODERN ART. SHE IS THE AUTHOR OF THE BOOK, DUST: EGYPT'S FORGOTTEN ARCHITECTURE. SHE IS KNOWN FOR MAKING THE BEST GIN & TONIC IN CAIRO.

**KARIM RAHMAN** LIVES FOR FAME, FOOD AND FASHION. HE IS A COLUMNIST AT CAIROSCENE. WRITING IS A MEANS WITH WHICH HE PAYS THE BILLS. HE ALSO LIKES WRITING BIOS IN THE THIRD PERSON.

**MARIAM SAADELDIN** WAS BORN AND RAISED IN CAIRO IN THE LATE SEVENTIES. FROM A VERY YOUNG AGE, SHE SHOWED AN INTEREST IN ARTS AND ACTING. SHE GRADUATED FROM THE CINEMA INSTITUTE AND HAS BEEN A FILMMAKER EVER SINCE.

**HUSSEIN EL SHAFIE** WAS ONCE A DOCTOR, TRIED TO BECOME A LAWYER AND ENDED UP WORKING IN COMMUNITY OUTREACH FOR HARASSMAP BUT SECRETLY ALL HE WANTS IS TO SING OPERA AND PLAY WITH HIS DOGS IN SINAI.

**NICHOLAS SIMCIK ARESE** IS A FREELANCE GEOGRAPHER, A FAKE ARCHITECT, AND A DOCTORAL CANDIDATE AT ST ANTONY'S COLLEGE, OXFORD. FOR THE PAST YEAR HE HAS BEEN LIVING IN SUBURBAN CAIRO WITH A GROUP OF SLUM-DWELLERS, SQUATTING A MIDDLE-CLASS GATED COMMUNITY.

**OLIVIA STERLING** HAS STUDIED POLITICAL SCIENCES AND ARAB CULTURE IN BRUSSELS. SHE NOW LIVES IN CAIRO WHERE SHE STUDIES ARABIC AND DOES RESEARCH ABOUT WOMEN'S ISSUES. OLIVIA ALSO ENJOYS THE EGYPTIAN ARTISTIC AND MUSICAL SCENE. SHE ENTERED THE ARABIC OUD HOUSE IN NOVEMBER 2012 WHERE SHE HAS BEEN STUDYING MUSIC AND "SAZ" UNTIL NOW.

**LAURA EL-TANTAWY** IS AN EGYPTIAN PHOTOGRAPHER LIVING BETWEEN CAIRO AND LONDON. SHE WAS BORN IN WORCESTERSHIRE, ENGLAND TO EGYPTIAN PARENTS AND GREW UP BETWEEN SAUDI ARABIA AND EGYPT. HER WORK HAS BEEN RECOGNISED ACROSS SEVERAL INTERNATIONAL PLATFORMS INCLUDING 2013 FINALIST PHE OJODEPEZ AWARD FOR HUMAN VALUES, 2013 WINNER CORTONA ON THE MOVE OFF CIRCUIT, 2013 HM FOTOVISURA GRANT AS WELL AS BEING SELECTED IN 2012 IN FOAM MAGAZINE'S ANNUAL TALENT EDITION, 2012.

**STEPH VON REISWITZ** IS AN ARTIST AND ILLUSTRATOR LIVING AND WORKING IN LONDON. A FAN OF MYSTERIOUS NARRATIVES, FILM NOIR, AND BLACK HUMOUR, STEPH HAS EXHIBITED WIDELY. SHE IS ALSO PART OF LONDON ART COLLECTIVE LE GUN.

**HANDE YALNIZOGLU + IASON ATHANASIADIS** : HANDE WRITES AND IASON PHOTOGRAPHS. THOUGH SUPPOSEDLY SWORN ENEMIES BY VIRTUE OF BEING BORN ON OPPOSITE SIDES OF THE AEGEAN, THEY DO SHARE SOME THINGS: ISTANBUL AS THEIR HOMETOWN, A PASSION FOR CAIRO AND A FASCINATION WITH EXPLORING THE UNCHARTED AND THE DISAPPEARING IN THE MIDDLE EAST. THOUGH ENGLISH IS THEIR COMMON LANGUAGE, WHETHER THEY'RE IN MOROCCO, UZBEKISTAN, AFGHANISTAN OR YEMEN THEY CAN GET BY IN ARABIC, GREEK, PERSIAN AND TURKISH.

**MAJA WADIN** IS A VIDEO JOURNALIST AND PHOTOGRAPHER WHO HAS WORKED FOR EL MASRY AL YOUM AND AHRAM ONLINE. SHE IS HALF SUDANESE AND HALF CROATIAN, BUT ALL OF HER LOVES EGYPT.